Reflections on the Posthuman in International Relations

The Anthropocene, Security and Ecology

EDITED BY

CLARA EROUKHMANOFF & MATT HARKER

ii

E-INTERNATIONAL
RELATIONS
PUBLISHING

E-International Relations
www.E-IR.info
Bristol, England
2017

ISBN 978-1-910814-31-4 (paperback)
ISBN 978-1-910814-32-1 (e-book)

Production: Michael Tang
Cover Image: (tbd)

A catalogue record for this book is available from the British Library

E-IR Edited Collections

Series Editors: Stephen McGlinchey, Marianna Karakoulaki and Agnieszka Pikulicka-Wilczewska

Editorial Assistance: Cameran Clayton, Edward Hovsepyan, Majer Ma and Tony Martel

E-IR's Edited Collections are open access scholarly books presented in a format that preferences brevity and accessibility while retaining academic conventions. Each book is available in digital and print versions and is published under a Creative Commons CC BY-NC 4.0 license. As E-International Relations is committed to open access in the fullest sense, free electronic versions of all of our books, including this one, are available on the E-International Relations website.

Find out more at: http://www.e-ir.info/publications

About the E-International Relations website

E-International Relations (www.E-IR.info) is the world's leading open access website for students and scholars of international politics, reaching over 3 million unique readers. E-IR's daily publications feature expert articles, blogs, reviews and interviews – as well as student learning resources. The website is run by a registered non-profit organisation based in Bristol, England and staffed with an all-volunteer team of students and scholars.

Abstract

This book exposes a much needed discussion on the interconnectedness between objects, organisms, machines and elemental forces. It seeks to disturb dogmatic ontologies that privilege human life and successfully questions the separation between the natural and human worlds. By doing so, the collection confronts, challenges, and energises discussion beyond International Relations' traditional territorial lines. By revealing the fragility of mainstream narratives of the 'human,' each author in this collection contributes to an unsettling vision of a posthuman world. Questions of what *the future* beyond the Anthropocene looks like pervasively infiltrate the collection and move away from a system that all too often relies on binary relationships. In contrast to this binary view of the world, *Reflections on the (post)human* (re)entagles the innate complexities found within the world and brings forward a plurality of views on posthumanism.

Editors

Clara Eroukhmanoff is a Lecturer in International Relations at London South Bank University. She has published in *Critical Studies on Terrorism*, *Critical Studies on Security* and *International Studies Review* and is currently working on her first monograph entitled 'The Securitisation of Islam after 9/11: Indirect Speech Acts and Affect in the United States' with Manchester University Press.

Matt Harker is a PhD Candidate at the Centre for the Study of Theory and Criticism at Western University in London, Canada. His work connects questions of biometric borders, landscapes, with questions of the social media, digital body, and conceptually understands these questions through the notion of exile. His work is grounded in meta-theoretical questions on the status of the contemporary body and theorises its condition as exilic.

Acknowledgements

We would first like to thank our contributors who have worked to produce a fascinating collaborative project and who put so much effort into making it an enjoyable experience for the editors. This project started when Clara attended a roundtable on 'posthuman security' at the European International Studies Association annual conference in 2015. She was stunned by the challenges that a posthuman agenda brought to the table. A first mini-series with the roundtable panellists (Audra Mitchell, Matt McDonald, Elke Schwarz and Carolin Kaltofen) was published online by E-International Relations. Enthusiasm about this mini-series, from our readers, our editor-in-Chief Stephen McGlinchey, and from the authors themselves, encouraged us to invite more people to the conversation. The authors who joined the mini-series (Olaf Corry, Cameron Harrington, Stefanie Fishel, Rafi Youatt, Delf Rothe and Darian Meacham) were not only willing to work with an already existing theme but also suggested original ideas that were central to this collection. A special thank you to the authors of the Introduction (Audra Mitchell and Matt McDonald) who had important input in organising this collection. We are very grateful to E-International Relations and in particular to Stephen McGlinchey, who has given us, the editors, so much support throughout the commissioning and editing process and who made sure to answer our constant questions promptly. Stephen was also right to point out that an edited collection always takes longer than it seems! Lastly, a thank you is owed to the E-International Relations team who always manages to spot the mistakes that we editors fail to notice.

Contributors

Olaf Corry is Associate Professor of International Relations at the University of Copenhagen. His books include *Constructing a Global Polity* (2013) and *Traditions and Trends in Global Environmental Politics: International Relations and the Earth* (2017) (with Hayley Stevenson). He has published articles on climate change, risk and security, environmental politics and social movements and International Relations theory in journals including Review of International Studies, Millennium, International Political Sociology and Global Environmental Change.

Stefanie Fishel is an Assistant Professor of Gender and Race at the University of Alabama. She is author of the book *The Microbial State: Global Thriving and the Body Politic.*

Cameron Harrington is an Assistant Professor in the School of Government and International Affairs, Durham University (beginning September 2017) and is a nonresident Research Associate in the Global Risk Governance Programme at the University of Cape Town. He is the co-author (with Clifford Shearing) of the book *Security in the Anthropocene: Reflections on Safety and Care*

Carolin Kaltofen is a post-doctoral research fellow at the Department of Science, Technology, Engineering and Public Policy (University College London), where she is heading a research project on 'Science Diplomacy', which maps the diverse interactions between the sciences and global governance. She has been teaching at the Department of International Politics at the University of Aberystwyth, where she obtained her doctorate degree in International Politics. Carolin's research is located at the intersection between metaphysics, materialisms, and the study of science and technology. She is particularly interested in how new technologies change the conditions of the political and being in the world.

Matt McDonald is a Reader in International Relations in the School of Political Science and International Studies at the University of Queensland. His research is in the area of critical theoretical approaches to security, and their application to environmental change and Australian foreign and security policy. He is the author of *Security, the Environment and Emancipation* (Routledge 2012) and co-author (with Anthony Burke and Katrina Lee-Koo) of *Ethics and Global Security* (Routledge 2014).

Darian Meacham is assistant professor of philosophy at Maastricht University, Maastricht, Netherlands, and Deputy Director for Responsible

Research and Innovation at BrisSynBio (a UK Research Council Funded Synthetic Biology Research Centre). He has published several articles and book chapters on human enhancement, and is currently interested in the social and political impact of automation technologies.

Audra Mitchell is the CIGI Chair in Global Governance and Ethics and Associate Professor at the Balsillie School of International Affairs, Wilfrid Laurier University, Canada. She has published widely in the areas of posthumanist IR, global ethics, large-scale harm, cosmology and violence. Her current research explores the ethics of global extinction.

Delf Rothe is a researcher and lecturer at the Institute for Peace Research and Security Policy in Hamburg, Germany. He received his PhD from the department of International Relations at the University of Hamburg in October 2014. Rothe has published widely on issues such as climate change and security discourse, visual security, resilience or environmental migration. He is the author of *Securitising Global Warming: A Climate of Complexity* (Routledge 2016),

Elke Schwarz is Lecturer in Politics and International Relations at the University of Leicester, UK. She holds a PhD from the London School of Economics in the ethics of international political violence. Her current research focuses on the ethical and political implications of lethal autonomous technologies and contemporary discourses on the posthuman.

Rafi Youatt is Assistant Professor of Politics at the New School for Social Research and Eugene Lang College. He is the author of *Counting Species: Biodiversity and Global Environmental Politics*, and has been published in journals including Millennium, Political Research Quarterly, Environmental Values, and International Political Sociology. He is currently completing a book on interspecies relations and international relations.

Contents

Introduction

Posthuman International Relations

MATT MCDONALD AND AUDRA MITCHELL

Preparing an introductory essay for an edited collection is never a straightforward enterprise. Managing the tasks of defining the scope of that collection, providing an outline of the contributions themselves and pointing to themes and intersections connecting the papers, as well as the questions they raise, is never a simple task. But in this instance, those challenges are much greater as a result of profound uncertainty and even contestation over the key term animating this collection and the expansive licence given to the authors of the thoughtful papers that follow. And, although the initial discussions on this theme emerged in a workshop in which a handful of the authors participated, they have grown and transformed across a series of discussions at several conferences in several countries and continents. In each iteration, new voices have joined to elaborate, contest and innovate on the initial themes.

Yet the scope of issues covered in these contributions, the significant licence given to contributors, and the relatively organic nature of the collection constitutes a key strength. So too does the variety amongst – and sometimes the productive tension between – interpretations, conceptualizations and arguments advanced in these interventions constitute an important contribution to existing debates. A discussion of the posthuman and its relationship to the study of international relations cannot be narrowly defined, nor can one voice (ours or a specified contributor's) be allocated the task of providing the definition of the posthuman or the other set of concepts addressed here: security, ecology, anthropocentrism or the Anthropocene. All are sites of debate themselves, and raise questions about what the interrogation of 'the human' and 'humanity's' relationship to other beings mean for the study and practice of international relations in the contemporary context. As such, they are rightly points of intellectual animation and contestation. And as Audra Mitchell notes in the first essay to follow, it is entirely appropriate that conversations about the posthuman and IR, here or in other contexts, should aim primarily to recognise and raise such questions rather than claim to provide definitive answers to them.

The 'posthuman turn' in the study of international relations, a phrasing certain to raise eyebrows and possibly ire amongst some IR scholars, essentially asks us to reflect critically on the role of humanity in the contemporary global context. More specifically, this provocation asks us to defamiliarise mainstream narratives of 'humanity' so that it is possible to better understand how it is constructed, performed and protected. Given rapid and far-reaching technological development, unprecedented environmental change, and more broadly the profoundly transnational nature of key challenges confronting the earth, this approach asks whether we can continue to work with implicit but powerful modern conceptions of a humanity separated from nature.[1] This question arises even before recognition of the profound threat now posed to other living beings or future generations – of humans and nonhumans alike - or the challenges posed by recognising and engaging non-living beings in the realm of ethics and security. Clearly, these moves raise a big set of questions. But for us and for many of the contributors here, those questions loom large (and indeed become urgent and necessary) in the context of the Anthropocene: the argument that the earth has entered a new geological era in which humans themselves have become the dominant influence on the conditions of planetary existence. As Delf Rothe's contribution notes, the Anthropocene does not in itself dictate an appropriate or even likely politics of response. However, given the impact of the ecological, social and political changes associated with this proposed era, it *should* force us to reflect on some of the key assumptions and guiding principles of IR, in theory and in practice.

The contributions that follow address many of these crucial questions. Few, if any, are entirely *new* questions. Grappling with the nature-human divide in social and ecological thought has a long history (see Eckersley 1992), and questions have long been asked about how IR has been constructed to confine its analyses to (imagined communities of) humans, assumed to be separate from a posited 'natural world' (Anderson 1983; Saurin 1996). The nature of the contributions made here, however, is distinctive in drawing together a new generation of scholars who are bringing these questions to bear on the most pressing ecological, political, security and ethical challenges facing the planet. In so doing, they draw on discourses that traverse the social sciences and humanities. For instance, several contributors are inspired by the 'new materialisms' (see Bennett 2010; Connolly 2011; Coole

---

[1]   Indeed posthuman accounts reject the concept of 'nature' as a human construct that precisely serves to separate humanity from the conditions of its existence. See Morton 2007.

and Frost 2011), which urge attunement to the lively property of materials. Others focus on articulations of the animals, plants and other nonhuman life forms that are co-implicated in the project of earthly survival, and that challenge traditional concepts of security, violence and threat (see Cudworth and Hobden 2011; Mitchell 2014). Meanwhile, some of the authors represented in this volume draw on object-oriented ontologies (Harman 2005; Bogost 2012) to explore how objects of all kinds construct and constrain existence beyond the boundaries of 'human' agency. Many of the contributions to this volume think alongside pioneering work in science and technology studies (Latour 2013; Stengers 2005; 2011) and, in particular, feminist approaches to this field (Haraway 2008; Barad 2007). The range of approaches, methodologies and philosophical frameworks discussed here demonstrate the diversity of ways in which 'posthumanisms' are articulated to challenge the core concepts and assumptions of IR.

Despite this diversity, at least two key themes suggest themselves across the contributions to follow. First, and especially for those contributors engaging directly with the question of environmental change, the relationship between anthropocentrism and ecocentrism looms large. Most strikingly, and perhaps surprisingly, in engaging this relationship in IR and even in locating themselves in a set of conversations about the posthuman, none of the contributors want to wholly reject one in favour of another. While all the contributors universally reject dominant forms of anthropocentrism, they vary both in their sense of the possibility or desirability of wholly moving beyond an anthropocentric frame. Instead, many of the interventions included in this volume seek re-articulations of the relations between humans and other beings that can mitigate the uncritical domination of the latter by the former. Similarly, while all of the authors in this volume express support in some form for moving towards increasing recognition of the embeddedness of humanity in nature, there is a notable sense of scepticism about the prospect of pure modes of ecocentrism. Reasons for this scepticism range from the analytical to the political (see Rafi Youatt's contribution), with Olaf Corry pointing to the intuitive appeal but limited political purchase of a position in which human society is viewed as 'dispensable to the Earth'. While Carolin Kaltofen (this volume) suggests that this ambivalence about ecocentrism may indeed challenge the extent to which contributions can genuinely be labelled 'posthuman', most endorse an expansion of human registers, care and consideration in reorienting attention *towards* an ecological perspective.

Second, and following the above, another key theme is that of relationality. All contributors, in different ways, challenge the tendency in IR to isolate entities and variables to make sweeping claims about 'the international' that ignore or obscure other kinds of relations. This is particularly evident in Cameron Harrington's discussion, drawing on feminist thought, of the desirability of an ethics of care that focuses on the relationship between the particular and the universal. It is evident, too, in Elke Schwarz's call to recognise and interrogate the nature of the relationship between humanity and technology, which profoundly challenges accounts of security weaponry that view these simply as objects employed by users. For contributors to this volume, profound and often deeply complex interrelationships- between people and objects; people and people; people and other living beings- necessitate new ways of thinking and engaging IR. This extends too, for Stefanie Fishel and Matt McDonald in particular, to the need for a radical reorientation of political practice, norms and institutions to respond adequately to the political cul-de-sacs dominant accounts of IR have taken us down so far (see also Burke et al. 2014; 2016).

The contributions that follow are grouped in two parts. Part 1 is themed around a theoretical discussion of the 'human', the 'posthuman' and 'posthumanism', while Part 2 contains contributions analysing ecology, non-human species and the Anthropocene. Neither parts, nor contributions within them, are wholly distinct from each other. While these broad thematic signposts are intended to help orient the reader, the deliberately significant scope of this volume and the licence given to contributors ensures that as many intersections occur between parts as within them.

In the first contribution to follow, the first in Part 1 of the volume, Audra Mitchell reflects on scholarship and debates around posthuman security in international relations networks to date. Noting controversy about the scope, role and desirability of both the 'posthuman' and 'security', her intervention points to both key axes of an evolving debate and avenues for future research. She ultimately makes a case for a 'reflexive anthropo-centredness', and suggests that future research in this space could benefit from drawing more on postcolonial theory, Indigenous knowledges and increased engagement with the planetary dimension of posthuman security. In the subsequent contribution, Carolin Kaltofen explores key conceptualisations and uses of the 'posthuman' in IR thought. Her paper situates interventions on the 'posthuman' in terms of different (and at times contradictory) philosophical and theoretical traditions, noting ultimately that much scholarship purporting to engage with the posthuman is better understood as an attempt to rearticulate humanism, albeit often in progressive ways. Her contribution compels us to drill deeper and reflect on the traditions and assumptions upon which claims are made, regarding posthumanism and IR scholarship more broadly.

The third contribution in this section, by Elke Schwarz, returns to the more specific theme of 'posthuman security', though in the process raises large questions about conceptions of humanity in IR. Using the example of new technologies of war and security, she points to the ways in which such technology needs to be viewed as more than a mere tool for the pursuit of security controlled by humans, instead raising important questions about how we conceive of ethics in war and even how conceptions of humanity might be affected or altered by the pursuit and use of technology. Rafi Youatt's contribution takes a step further back, reflecting on the anthropocentrism often depicted as serving a fundamental rationale for the posthuman turn and a key impediment to progressive human-nature relations. His analysis here suggests the need to question the simple human-nature binary, in the process pointing to the realities of multiple forms of humanity and humanness and multiple forms and dynamics of nature. It also asks broader questions about distinctions made between living and non-living objects and beings.

The final contribution in Part 1, by Stefanie Fishel, develops a three act structure for exploring the posthuman in IR. Developing the performative theme, her paper makes the case that we should focus less on the condition of the post-human than on the process of post-humanising, which must entail a shift away from traditional forms of anthropocentrism which separate humans from nature. She concludes with a call to arms for the reconstruction of humanity and the discipline (and practice) of IR to address contemporary global challenges, building in the process on her recent work elsewhere (Burke et al. 2016).

The first paper of Part 2, by Matt McDonald, deals most directly with the concept of security. In this paper he makes the case that the increasing tendency to securitise climate change raises important questions about *how* the security-climate relationship is understood. Pointing to the limits and pathologies of discourses that emphasise the preservation of national, international and even human security, he makes a case for endorsing and pursuing a discourse of climate security oriented towards long-term ecosystem resilience, in the process encouraging practices focused on mitigation and the rights and needs of future generations and other living beings. This security focus is also prominent in Cameron Harrington's contribution, which similarly explores the type of sensibility that should inform a more progressive approach to unprecedented environmental change in the context of the Anthropocene. Here he makes a case, drawing on feminist thought, for an ethics of care in informing how we view security in posthuman terms. This, he suggests, is attentive to relations between the particular and the universal and recognises our entanglement in the experiences and vulnerability of those beyond our immediate horizon.

Delf Rothe's contribution simultaneously continues the security theme while returning to the question raised by Carolin Kaltofen of the assumptions underpinning existing scholarship in IR on the posthuman. In particular, he focuses on the meaning given to the Anthropocene. Here, he argues that scholarship on the Anthropocene frequently assumes that recognition of this new geological era will serve as a trigger for a reconfigured and progressive relationship between nature and humanity. In the process, he suggests that such scholarship insufficiently acknowledges the multiple meanings that might be given to the Anthropocene itself, and crucially the set of varied practices these may in turn encourage. In this sense, he argues for a richer sociological account of the Anthropocene and meanings attributed to it, in order to develop a richer and more realistic account of the ethics and politics of security in the context of the Anthropocene.

Finally, Olaf Corry's intervention examines the role of 'nature' in international relations thought. Reflecting directly on how IR has engaged 'nature' or 'the environment' over time, Corry suggests that IR had ultimately forgotten about rediscovering nature since World War II. Turning his attention to the question of how IR *should* engage the human-nature/social-natural distinction, he ultimately makes the case for preserving an analytical distinction between the two while recognising the possibility for dialectical 'progress' associated with changing conceptions of both the natural world and the human condition.

The contributions to this volume are challenging and thought-provoking, often asking fundamental questions about the way those interested in IR can and should think about politics, ethics, security, unprecedented environmental change and technological development, humanity and the human-nature divide. These questions could scarcely be larger, and this volume certainly does not provide definitive answers to all of them. Indeed, in some ways, it raises as many questions as it resolves – but they are questions worth asking if IR is to enable and influence meaningful forms of political practice in the face of planetary challenges. And while this volume identifies numerous pathologies in IR scholarship and global political practice, it also points towards alternative politics, ethical registers and analytical frameworks better suited to face up to these challenges.

References

Anderson, Benedict. 1983. *Imagined Communities: Reflections on the origins and spread of nationalism.* London: Verso.

Barad, Karen. 2007. *Meeting the Universe Halfway*. Durham, NC: Duke University Press, 2007.

Bennett, Jane. 2010. *Vibrant Matter: A Political Ecology of Things*. Durham, NC: Duke University Press, 2010.

Bogost, Ian. 2012. *Alien Phenomenology, or, What It's Like to Be A Thing*. Minneapolis: University of Minnesota Press.

Burke, Anthony, Katrina Lee-Koo and Matt McDonald. 2016. "Ethics and Global Security"*Journal of Global Security Studies* 1(1): 64-79.

Burke, Anthony, Katrina Lee-Koo and Matt McDonald. 2014. *Ethics and Global Security: A Cosmopolitan Approach*. Abingdon: Routledge.

Connolly, William. 2011. *A World of Becoming*. Durham, NC: Duke University Press.

Coole, Diana and Samantha Frost, eds. 2010. *New Materialisms: Ontology, Agency and Politics*. Durham, NC: Duke University Press.

Cudworth, Erika and Stephen Hobden. 2011. *Posthuman International Relations: Complexity, Ecologism and Global Politics*. London: Zed Books.

Eckersley, Robyn. 1992. *Environmentalism and Political Theory*. New York: SUNY Press.

Haraway, Donna. 2008. *When Species Meet*. Minneapolis: University of Minnesota Press.

Harman, Graham. 2005. *Guerrilla Metaphysics: Phenomenology and the Carpentry of Things*. Peru, Illinois: Open Court Publishing.

Latour, Bruno. 2013. *An Inquiry Into Modes of Existence*. Cambridge: Harvard University Press.

Mitchell, Audra. 2013. "Only Human? A Worldly Approach to Security" *Security Dialogue*, 45(1): 5-21.

Morton, Timothy. 2007. *Ecology without Nature*. Cambridge MA: Harvard University Press.

Saurin, Julian. 1996. "International relations, social ecology and the globalisation of environmental change" in *Environment and International Relations*, edited by John Vogler and Mark Imber. London: Routledge.

Stengers, Isabelle. 2005. "A Cosmopolitical Proposal" in *Making Things Public: Atmospheres of Democracy*, edited by Bruno Latour and Peter Weibel. Cambridge, MA: MIT Press.

Stengers, Isabelle (trans. Robert Bononno). 2011. *Cosmopolitics II*. Minneapolis: University of Minnesota Press.

Part One

HUMAN,
THE POSTHUMAN,
POSTHUMANISM

1

'Posthuman Security': Reflections from an Open-ended Conversation

AUDRA MITCHELL

A couple of years ago, I invited a group of scholars (including several of the authors in this volume) to get together and share their views on something called 'posthuman security'. While we all had different disciplinary backgrounds, expertise, questions and commitments, we shared the intuition that international security is not solely a matter of securing human lives and bodies. Instead, we contended that diverse beings other than humans are implicated in the conditions of (in)security. With this in mind, we wanted to think collectively about what the notion of 'security' means in worlds intersected and co-constituted by various kinds of beings: humans, other organisms, machines, elemental forces, diverse materials – plus hybrids, intersections and pluralities of all of the above (and more). In turn, we wanted to think about what the 'posthuman' means when we bring it into the realm of security. For instance, does embracing a more-than-human or post-human ontology mean giving up on notions of security as stability, sustainability or resilience? On the other hand, does embracing such concepts force one back into a humanism that reinforces rigid and exclusive understandings of what 'humanity' is, and what is worthy of being secured? Over the last two years, we have met to hash out these issues with a widening group of interlocutors in workshops and panels in the UK, Australia, Italy and the US. So what kinds of insight have these discussions inspired?

One remarkable aspect of the discussions was the breadth and range of positions that are identified as 'posthuman' or 'posthumanist'. In her recent E-IR piece, Elke Schwarz (this volume) notes this diversity, but suggests that posthumanism can be approached largely in terms of transhumanism, hybridity and the cyborg. This is indeed an important current in posthumanist thinking, and one that, as Schwarz suggests, has important implications for traditional security concerns such as the conduct of warfare and the distribution of agency in violence. On the other hand, many contemporary posthumanists are inspired by engagements with the liveliness and quirkiness of matter and its implications for ontology, agency and causation. They draw on sources such as new materialism (Coole and Frost 2011; Bennett, 2010; Connolly, 2011) and the politics of affect (Massumi 2015; Protevi 2013). Carolin Kaltofen's work draws on these sources to examine the emergence of hybrid posthumans in the worlds of the virtual and sonic warscapes. Still other participants in our discussion are concerned with how thinking in ecological terms transforms perspectives on what it means to be 'human' – and what it means to be 'secure'. For instance, the work of Erika Cudworth and Stephen Hobden (2014, 2015) examines the implications of animal bodies and subjectivities in warfare. In a similar light, Stefanie Fishel's work on the subjectivity of dolphins and Matt McDonald's (this volume) new framework for 'ecological security' each call for profound transformations of the perceived subjects of security and their influence in international law and norms (see also Mitchell 2014b). Rafi Youatt's (2014) work on international regimes of biodiversity show how this category has become progressively securitised, altering ideas of what 'life' is and what should be protected. Meanwhile, other authors are concerned with the agentic role of the 'things' we tend to construe as rigid and lifeless, in particular, their ability to provoke human thought and action, structure violence and create disruption (see Grove 2014). Even this wide variety of approaches only scratches the surface of the perspectives that are expressed under the rubric of posthumanism or 'posthuman security'. These terms do not refer to 'theory' or 'framework', but rather to a swarm of resonating, sometimes intersecting and often conflicting lines of thought.

In this context, one of the most prevalent aspects of our discussions on 'posthuman security' is the tension between identifying convergences in these contributions and maintaining the openness of the discourse. To my mind, one of the most promising and radical aspects of these discussions has been their stubborn resistance to resolution. However, the inertia of scholarly debate tends to push such discussions towards the articulation of definitions and particular 'projects' or frameworks. Our struggles with this tension have produced a number of rich debates.

One of the most salient of these debates surrounds whether or not 'the human' has a place in 'posthuman' security. At a 2015 roundtable discussion on the subject at the European International Studies Association Convention in Sicily, there was significant contention over whether or not the visions of 'posthuman security' presented by various contributors were radical enough. Some of our interlocutors expressed the view that anything short of the total elimination of anthropocentric thinking from IR simply reproduced existing paradigms, in particular, the ontology of liberal capitalism. Others contended that it is impossible – and undesirable – to excise 'humanity' entirely from a discussion of security or politics more generally. I have a great deal of sympathy for the latter perspective. Elsewhere, I have advocated the transformation of security thinking around the principle of 'weak anthropocentrism' – a position which acknowledges the embeddedness of humans in complex worlds co-constituted by diverse beings (Mitchell 2014a). Perhaps a better term, in fact, is 'reflexive anthropo-centredness': the ability to be mindful of the various ways that one might be figured, conditioned or disciplined as 'human', and how they affect one's sense of relationality, ethics, politics and co-existence.

From these perspectives, 'security' cannot be understood as a good or status that accrues to bounded, separated, 'purely human' beings. Instead, concepts of (in)security, violence and harm must be understood in relation to distinct, irreplaceable worlds and the relations that bind them. These approaches also highlight how existing logics of security function as a set of ethical boundaries that isolate a narrowly-defined category of 'humanity' from the diverse worlds that co-constitute it (Mitchell 2016b). Ironically, this strategy renders 'humanity' less secure in two major ways. First, it widens the gulf between the 'human' being and the relations that sustain it, as well as knowledge of how to maintain them. Second, by illustrating the constructed nature of 'humanity' as an ethical category, it opens this category up to further contractions and destabilizations. From traditional security perspectives that focus on maintaining 'humanity-as-it-is', this is deeply problematic. However, some modes of posthumanism suggest that it is precisely the destabilization of 'humanity' that can make it possible to transcend rigid categories such as gender, race and sexuality (Braidotti 2013; Mitchell 2016).

Viewed from this angle, it is not possible to entirely escape the constructs, norms and shared experiences that help to define one's life as a human. However, the idea of what it means to *be (post)human* can be transformed by a deep engagement with alternative ontologies, cosmologies and multiple, co-constituting worlds. This suggests that between the two extremes suggested by our interlocutors – a radical, eliminative posthumanism and a relapse into unreflective humanism – there exists a wide space of relations. It is these (international) relations that our discussions probe. In this sense, our discussions are post-human*ist.* That is, they situate themselves in a range of critical positions in relation to human*ism*, particularly the dominant variety that underpins international frameworks such as international norms of humanitarianism (Mitchell 2014b). But they are not *anti*-human: they embrace the deep plurality of ways in which one can be, or become, (post)human. They also encourage the practice of reflecting critically on the category of 'humanity' better to grasp the nature of violence, harm and crisis.

Another flashpoint in our discussions concerns the concept of 'security'. In particular, various contributors have asked whether it makes any sense to continue pursuing security in radically relational worlds disrupted by global crises such as climate change and mass extinction. Moreover, the emergence of hybrids, cyborgs and transhumans suggests that the entire category of humanity is vulnerable to dissolution – along with the frameworks of law, ethics and global norms it underpins. It is clear from our discussions that security as stasis is not feasible: it does not match with the exigencies of a dynamic, entangled and volatile earth. Indeed, one of the major arguments included in the recent 'Planet Politics Manifesto' (Burke et al. 2016) is that existing frameworks and assumptions of international politics do not 'match the earth', and must be rebuilt if they are to do so.

At the same time, extending existing logics of security 'beyond the human' to penetrate additional dimensions of earthly co-existence threatens to compound regimes of biopolitical control. The recent work of Mark Evans and Julian Reid (2013) illustrates how fear over climate change and mass extinction has fuelled neo-liberal modes of sovereignty rooted in the production and 'resilience' of bare, often commodified, life. A good example of this can be found in contemporary conservation strategies that convert 'biodiversity' into registers of financial value and monetary instruments – including 'biodiversity derivatives' (Mandel et al. 2010) – as a response to the threat of extinction. Such practices respond to the annihilation of worlds and life-forms by attempting scientifically to manage the processes of (bare) life and death. In so doing, they condemn all forms and expressions of life to existence in 'survival mode', compelled to conform to a specific understanding of 'life' and its persistence through time.

As this example suggests, there are strong critical reasons to resist existing drives to envelop more and more aspects of the more-than-human within existing security discourses. Our discussions have stressed the need for attention to the double-edged sword of making security 'more-than-human'. However, they have also identified important visions for opening up the meaning of security. For instance, Tony Burke's (2015) recent work on 'security cosmopolitanism' offers an ambitious new vision of insecurity as 'processes that threaten or cause serious harm to human beings, communities, and ecosystems; harm to their structures of living, dignity, and survival'. His work calls for the transformation of understandings of security to become responsive to the nature and dynamics of vibrant, diverse systems – human, organic, material, technological – across time and space. It suggests that the kind of 'security' that might emerge from a serious engagement with posthumanist thought may not resemble anything like traditional and existing paradigms. In this sense, perhaps this line of thought would better be called 'post-human post-security'.

So it is safe to say that most of the contributors to this discussion are not fully comfortable with or committed to either 'posthumanism' or 'security'. Why, then, do we all find ourselves repeatedly drawn to engage with them, juxtapose them and explore their resonances? I think this is largely because their intersection opens up a series of problems, questions and critiques that break from established paradigms and hold the promise of alternative futures. So where are discussions of posthuman security going next?

While I can only speak from my own perspective, I see a number of avenues in which these discourses can continue to break ground. First, discussions of posthumanism and security can engage more robustly with postcolonial theory (an issue around which Cudworth and Hobden's work has broken ground). In particular, there is considerable promise in exploring how highly normative categories of 'humanity' are implicated in the construction of exclusive categories such as species and race. To give just one example, Achille Mbembe's *On the Postcolony* (2002) brilliantly articulates how the category of animality has underpinned colonial violence against humans and other animals. More recently, he has called on humans to address the Anthropocene by 'see[ing] ourselves clearly, not as an act of secession from the rest of the humanity, but in relation to ourselves and to other selves with whom we share the universe' (Mbembe 2014, 15). There is huge scope to identify the shared logic of arbitrary division and hierarchy that underpin regimes of violence against any and all beings that fail to fit within mainstream norms of 'humanity'.

However, 'posthumanist' thought also needs to engage more directly with its unacknowledged *debt* to Indigenous philosophy and ways of thinking. As my collaborator Zoe Todd (2014) has pointed out, new materialist and post-humanist modes of thought ignore and often efface the roots of many of their key tenets – profound relationality, multi-species community and an ecological ethic – in Indigenous philosophy and thought. 'Indigenous thought' is not a single, homogenous category. Instead, it is an admittedly inadequate way of signalling towards the hugely plural, singular bodies of thought, cosmologies, philosophies and lived knowledge kept and created by Indigenous peoples across the earth and over millennia. While none of these ways of knowing can be reduced to any other, some ideas – for instance, the co-constitution of beings – resonate across them. Juanita Sundberg (2014, 38) has recently critiqued 'posthumanist' thought on the basis that it 'enacts the world as universe, meaning the ontological assumption of a singular reality or nature, about which different cultures offer distinct interpretations'. Instead, if posthumanisms can recognise other worlds and cosmologies, this may open up new conversations across and amongst bodies of knowledge. In particular, by engaging seriously with plural forms of Indigenous thought, discussions of posthumanism and security can move towards a more self-critical understanding of the cosmologies they espouse and the forms of violence they might unwittingly condone. In addition, they might gain an appreciation of plural meanings of violence, harm and insecurity. I am exploring this pathway in my current work, which involves re-thinking the ethical dimensions of global extinction by engaging with plural Indigenous cosmologies and the communities who keep them. This involves thinking with contemporary Indigenous writers, artists and activists to theorise extinction, but also to understand its sources in large-scale forms of worlding associated with 'the global'.

Another direction which discussions of posthuman security can take is to engage more directly with the planet, and the specific conditions of (in) security on earth. This entails thinking about the elemental, geological and cosmological conditions of life on this planet. For instance, the work of geographer Nigel Clark (2011) urges humans to embrace the finite, deeply contingent existence furnished by an earth that is less dependent on them than they are on it. He claims that human existence is contingent upon conditions created by previous (largely extinct) life forms and by inhuman forces, both contemporary and temporally distant. From this perspective, existence is a gift given to humans – and to *all* existent earthlings. Instead of struggling to secure it at all costs, and resenting the finitude that comes along with it, he argues that humans should embrace an ethic of gratitude towards the Earth. This may include welcoming new worlds and beings – for instance, transhumans, hybrids or post-human organisms – that threaten the boundaries of humanity and endanger existing forms of human life. From this perspective, engaging with the post-human may actually involve thinking a world without humans, or a world in which existing modes of human life are no longer possible. That, in turn, requires relinquishing the idea of security as perpetual existence to be ensured at all costs (see Mitchell 2017). For many theorists of security, this might appear to be a frightening and counter-productive stance. However, along with the renunciation of security-as-we-know it would come the freedom to celebrate and cherish the 'gift' of existence on a volatile planet. How these insights and ethical vocations might re-shape understandings of security and global ethics cries out for further discussion.

These are a few of the new directions that the discussion of 'posthuman security' can take in its impulse to explore the intersections of humans and the diverse, transforming worlds we help to constitute. The strength of this discourse is that it places both of its key terms – 'posthumanism' and 'security' – in constant question, and stubbornly refuses closure into any particular vision of either. Indeed, although I have outlined some of the currents of this discussion so far, and some future paths it might follow, the conversation remains open to new and different ideas, critiques, interventions and futures. My account of these discourses should not be misconstrued as an 'expert' attempt to define them. Instead, these are the reflections of a participant-observer in an ongoing conversation that, I hope, will continue to create controversy, provoke arguments, frustrate academic expectations, spark collaborations and engender plural visions. Consider this your invitation to join us.

References

Bennett, Jane. 2010. *Vibrant Matter: A Political Ecology of Things*. Durham, NC: Duke University Press.

Burke, Anthony. 2015. "Security Cosmopolitanism 2.0" Global Theory. Available online at: https://worldthoughtworldpolitics.wordpress. com/2015/10/08/security-cosmopolitanism-2-0/. Accessed 17 May 2017.

Burke, Anthony, Stefanie Fishel, Audra Mitchell, Simon Dalby and Daniel J. Levine. 2016. "Planet Politics: A Manifesto from the End of IR" *Millennium Journal of International Studies* 44 (3): 494-523.

Clark, Nigel. 2011. Inhuman Nature: Sociable Life on a Dynamic Planet. London: Sage.

Connolly, William. 2011. *A World of Becoming*. Durham, NC: Duke University Press.

Cudworth, Erika, and Stephen Hobden. 2014. "Civilization and the Domination of the Animal" *Millennium Journal of International Studies* 42 (3): 746-66.

Cudworth, Erika, and Stephen Hobden. 2015. "The Posthuman Way of War." *Security Dialogue* 46 (6): 513-29.

Coole, Diana, and Samantha Frost, eds. 2010. *New Materialisms: Ontology, Agency and Politics*. Durham, NC: Duke University Press.

Connolly, William. 2011. *A World of Becoming*. Durham, NC: Duke University Press.

Evans, Brad, and Julian Reid. 2014. *Resilient Life.* Cambridge: Polity Press.

Fishel, Stefanie. "Posthuman Personhoods: Corporations, Dolphins and Ecological Security" Posthuman Security, available online at: https:// posthumansecurity.wordpress.com/animals/. Accessed 17 May 2017.

Grove, Jairus Victor, 2014. "Ecology as Critical Security Method" *Critical Studies on Security* 2 (3): 366-9.

Mandel, James T., C. Josh Donlan, and Jonathan Armstrong. 2010. "A Derivative Approach to Endangered Species Conservation" *Frontiers in Ecology and the Environment* 8 (1): 44-49.

Massumi, Brian. 2015. *The Politics of Affect.* Cambridge: Polity.

Mbembe, Achille. 2014. "Decolonising Knowledge and the Question of the Archive" pp.1-29. Available online at: http://wiser.wits.ac.za/system/files/ Achille%20Mbembe%20-%20Decolonizing%20Knowledge%20and%20 the%20Question%20of%20the%20Archive.pdf. Accessed 15 January, 2016.

Mbembe, Achille. 2012. *On the Postcolony.* California: University of California Press.

Mitchell, Audra. 2014a. "Only Human? Towards Worldly Security" *Security Dialogue* 41 (1): 1-23.

Mitchell, Audra. 2014b. *International Intervention in a Secular Age: Re-enchanting Humanity.* London: Routledge.

Mitchell, Audra. 2016. "Posthuman Security/Ethics" in Anthony Burke and Jonna Nyman, eds. *Ethical Security Studies*, London: Routledge.

Mitchell, Audra. 2017. "Is IR Going Extinct?" *The European Journal of International Relations* 23 (1): 3-25

Protevi, John, 2013. *Life, War, Earth: Deleuze and the Sciences.* Minneapolis: University of Minnesota Press.

Sundberg, Juanita. 2014. "Decolonising Posthumanist Geographies" *Cultural Geographies* 21 (1): 33-47.

Todd, Zoe. 2014. "An Indigenous Feminist's Take on the Ontological Turn: 'Ontology' is Just Another Word for Colonization". Available online at: https:// zoeandthecity.wordpress.com/2014/10/24/an-indigenous-feminists-take-on-the-ontological-turn-ontology-is-just-another-word-for-colonialism/. Accessed 15 January 2016.

Viveiros de Castro, Eduardo, 2012. *Cosmologial Perspectivism in Amazonia and Elsewhere*. Manchester: HAU Network of Ethnographic Theory.

Youatt, Rafi, 2015. *Counting Species: Biodiversity in Global Environmental Politics*. University of Minnesota Press.

2

Between Radical Posthumanism and Weak Anthropocentrism: The Spectrum of Critical Humanism(s)

CAROLIN KALTOFEN

The increasing relevance of and interest in contending philosophies of materiality, often referred to as posthuman literature such as vital materialism, have inspired different strands of posthuman and post-anthropocentric thinking across the social sciences. In IR most of the posthuman issues, albeit not always labelled as such, are investigated under the analytic banner of speculative/new materialism, which increasingly makes reference to the 'posthuman'.[2] In this paper I explore different conceptions and uses of the posthuman in International Relations (IR). While the notion of the posthuman leads to fascinating new approaches to the dynamics of the international, this recent theoretical turn, especially the ways in which new materialist philosophies as an instance of the posthuman have been adopted in IR, is problematic due to its incoherence and ambiguity as a scholarship, discourse and concept. The overall engagement with these notional difficulties underlying the posthuman project leads to the suggestion that posthumanism(s) in IR 'is in fact weak anthropocentrism' (Mitchell 2014, 6).

Approaching Posthuman Dialogues

In order to understand the development of posthuman ideas in IR, it is

---

[2]   Prominent scholars working in this area are for example Diana Coole (2010), William Connolly (2011), Erika Cudworth and Stephen Hobden (2011), Audra Mitchell (2014) and Mike Bourne (2012).

necessary to distinguish between posthuman accounts in IR that draw on contemporary 'posthuman' philosophy and the latter philosophical works themselves. In broad strokes, primary philosophical investigations, which conceptualise life differently to the predominant humanist metaphysics, suggest that thinking beyond the human (as a species, as a body and as a subject) and its primacy in our conception and treatment of the world and the life unfolding within it, marks a fundamental break from previous understandings of being and practices of 'theoretical reason [that] is concept-bound' (Braidotti 2002, 2). While there are other factors that specify this new 'post', the two main characteristics of this turn are arguably ontological and epistemic. The ontological effort lies in acknowledging that the human may not be human after all, which calls to re-think existence and being in the world. The consequence is epistemic because if we assume that our being and becoming is different from what we previously thought (given that we are likely to be implicated in a posthuman life), we can no longer explain how we experience and think in conventional epistemological terms. Questioning the human body and subject far beyond its discursive and performative construction topples centuries of epistemological beliefs, triggering powerful theoretical resonances. Chasing the posthuman reveals a world that is entirely different to the one we know and have studied so far (Rutsky 2007). At least this is how the argument goes. In this sense, the enquiry into a posthuman condition is to revisit the very make-up and function of the world and life.

By reviewing different posthuman attempts, it becomes clear that there are various levels of posthuman-ness depending on the degree to which each conceptualisation strays away, indeed undermines, the human as a separate and independent form of life. Work by philosophers such as Gilles Deleuze and Manuel DeLanda inform the more radical end of the spectrum where bodies are not bound by skin, but rather flows of affect and intensities; where thought is not human in its origin, but non-local and pre-subjective, thereby toppling ideas of human consciousness and agency (DeLanda 1992; Deleuze 2001). *A body* and *a life* are mere material processes of self-emergence and self-organisation including a wide range of organic and non-organic materials. Generally speaking, the thought experiment of the posthuman seeks to undo the human category and conceive of being and becoming without reference to a human condition and Cartesian dualism. However, other understandings of the posthuman are less drastic and leave the physiological and neurological integrity of the human intact, representing the other end of the spectrum. The different degrees of posthuman-ness are rarely acknowledged and the majority of posthuman efforts in IR (may this be in security or other aspects of the political) are taking from the human-conservative end. However, the latter is problematic insofar as it is not quite clear why and how it is 'posthuman' at all. Furthermore, the emerging posthuman trend over the past years has lead to a posthuman discourse and turn/scholarship that 'comprises a rather heterogeneous and not always compatible set of theoretical positions' (Lundborg and Vaughan-Williams 2015, 4). It appears that most 'posthuman' approaches are merely cases of criticising either the role of the human, humanism or anthropocentrism or a combination thereof, but not so much human being/being human itself. As such, I briefly outline six different ways asking about the human(ism) in order to show that merely criticising the human is not a full posthuman move, especially in consideration of much more uncompromising ideas of the posthuman.

Different Traditions and Applications: Is the 'warrant for the death of Man' Posthumanism?

The increasing interdisciplinarity of academic practice makes it difficult to draw a clear distinction between materialist philosophies seeking to articulate a posthuman ontology and applications thereof in the social sciences, given that a considerable part of contemporary philosophy (especially continental philosophy) is happening across and between academic subjects. In this sense it is easier to approximate posthuman scholarship by distinguishing it from other works that problematise the givenness of the human. However, literature critical of the human or humanism in a conventional sense often work in different and unrelated ways and aspects. As elaborated in more detail below, voices critical of the human – which here are grouped together as critical humanism(s) for practical reasons – differ from each other and differ from posthuman ideas depending on the type of questions they are asking. Some strands are interested in problematising the role of the human in relation to other living beings and objects, while others are focused on the human body and subject in itself. Yet, the underlying assumption of 'a human' as a body and subject remains, so that it is only its dominance, self-alleged superiority, and privilege that needs to be corrected to include the previously marginalised (in which ever shape or form these appear). In light of this, the general argument is that while the criticism concerning the primacy of the human as a form of life and political actor is an important area of scholarship in and of itself, this is not always a posthuman effort as such. For example, criticising the centrality of the human in the theory and practice of security, is not a complete posthuman move.

Criticising Static Bourgeois Man

In the advent of critical humanism(s) – understood as different ways of asking about and challenging the human(ism) – one of the first ways in which the human came under scrutiny was regarding its assumed essence and its acclaimed dominant role in structuring/influencing life on earth (the epoch of the anthropocene). Especially earlier critical humanism attacks humans' primacy and supremacy through a logic of decentring man in the landscape of the anthropocene. Within this project of decentring, different attempts can be distinguished by the way in which they seek to remove the human from its dominant, centric position.[3] This line of criticism disagrees with humanism's essentialism that ignores (different aspects of) production, but not with the idea that there is an eventual end product of the human animal. Indeed, this criticism still holds that by looking at productive processes it is possible to *'find real men'* (Althusser 1976, 53). Hence, when located on the spectrum of posthuman-ness, this variant – often associated with Karl Marx's historical materialism – falls short of a posthuman ontology and instead lays the foundations for the development of critical humanism.[4]

Criticising Static Binaries and the Big Ism

It can be argued that later posthuman work was inspired by early critical humanism, such as Marx's historical materialism, that deconstructs man as an absolute departure point for political, historical, social and other enquiries. Questioning the role of the human (subject) in this way gained momentum as an intellectual project and agenda in the social sciences and continental philosophy, and we see two strands developing alongside and often in tandem with each other. One questions the centrality of the human at the level of the human and society, the other questions it at the level of humanity and intellectual traditions. Foucault's proclamation of the end of man in *The Order of Things* gave rise to serious possibilities of further decentring the human and, eventually, to deconstruct it as the main political and security referent. It meant that the human and in particular man was no longer treated as the measure of all things and used as the structuring device of, for example, society, politics or history (Braidotti 2013, 23); which differs from the way in which Marx sought to dismantle the primacy of man. Subsequent post-anthropocentric development in the Twentieth Century can be observed to occur at two levels: 1) at the level of biopolitics where the concern is with binaries and dichotomies, which focused on the displacement and blurring of boundaries that are routinely used in order to normalise, nationalise, gender, sex, globalise, or otherwise discipline living and nonliving bodies;[5] and 2) at the level of intellectual history as a more abstract and general critique, attacking conventional humanism as an intellectual practice itself for it maintains and furthers the awe of human superiority (based on its ability to

---

[3]   As seen in the works of Karl Marx and Louis Althusser, for example.

[4]   Nonetheless, this intellectual tradition initiates a decentring of the human from the centre of history and as its driving force by looking at other constitutive processes of the social.

[5]   As seen in Judith Butler's work, for example.

reason and to act morally and ethically), the human as moving towards perfection, and the normalcy this takes in explaining and justifying intellectual traditions. With regard to the first strand, it can be argued that decentring the human by blurring its own and other boundaries does not suggest a full posthuman ontology, but a type of critical human(ism) that is androgynous and hybrid. Rather than suggesting a posthuman alternative in a strict sense, this move offered the opportunity to open up spaces at the margins and those previously outside in our study of the international, challenging the ways in which we have written and have been written as privileged, whole and gendered humans into a binary and dichotomised world. Turning to the second type, then we are dealing with a decentring of the human from its privileged position through the vigorous critique on the entire phenomenon of the Western Canon, Enlightenment and modern philosophical practices. This variant seeks to undermine the rational human and to rid philosophy of 'all the "Humanist" rubbish that is brazenly being dumped into it' (Althusser quoted in Badmington 2004, 41). Yet, critique here is still pitched in terms of human phenomena embedded in a correlationist framework.[6] Sceptics articulate their criticism in reference to the humanist orbit and human limits, connecting their analysis to the human experience.[7] Given this, it would be a stretch to consider this type of critical humanism a form of posthumanism in the radical sense.

Cyborgs: An Ultrahuman Manifesto

Nonetheless, all three versions of re-structuring the landscape and epoch of the human significantly influenced the study of IR. And so the critical humanism of the postmodern was the ideal breeding ground for posthuman trends and discourse in the age of scientific and technological acceleration that fuelled debates about the abilities and limits of the human organism. The advance and availability of technology lead to question not only the status of reality, but also that of the human itself. Technology's increasing ubiquity in the Western way of life meant that the human body and subject got blended and mended with its supposedly non-natural environment. Depending on what technological determinism one subscribes to (whether instrumentalism or essentialism)[8] the body is either technologically extended, enhanced and

---

[6]   Quentin Meillassoux's explanation of correlationism holds that in a dualist understanding humans exist as sentient and cognisant beings-in-the-world, where it is impossible to speak about the world 'independent of thought or language' (Moulard-Leonard 2008, 4).

[7]   As seen in Foucault's discussions of power and discursive structures, Lacan's analysis of the signifier and the real as well as Derrida's discussions of the play of the signifier and the trace, and albeit to a lesser extent, Luhmann's work on social systems as communication systems (Bryant 2010).

[8]   For more see for example Daniel McCarthy's 'Technology and 'the International' or:

upgraded, or invaded and under attack. However, as R.L. Rutsky notes 'there is, in fact, nothing inherently posthuman about technological or genetic enhancements of the human body' as these approaches still start with human as the point-zero of departure. Furthermore, the dominance of the subject remains and it is only the boundaries of its body that is tampered with. Indeed, the cyborg and its technologically enhanced humanity is a reinforcement of the human and humanism 2.0. As tempting as it is to take the neuromancing cyborg as an icon of post-anthropocentrism, the form of life it describes is far removed from the posthuman in the initial philosophical sense.

More-than-Humans and Species Egalitarianism

Posthuman debates in IR, especially in security studies, are often associated with the increased impetus to go beyond the human in terms of species and to include non-human animals, living organisms and other organic components of our ecosystem into the analysis. These are dominant trends in critical ecology, animal studies and environmentalism that speak of non-humans, 'earthlings' and earth-others, and who thereby reject self-centred individualism.[9] The motivation of the more-than-human approach, especially as adopted in IR, is focused on the lively aspects of all beings, including our natural and non-natural environment (Cudworth and Hobden 2013). This scholarship frequently conceives of threats to other living things on earth as a security issue. While the more-than-human camp is hugely diverse, a large part of its posthuman inspired thought is an attack on '*the* fundamental anthropological dogma associated with humanism' of the humanity/animality dichotomy whereby the human escaped its animal and barbaric origin by dominating nature, transcending immediate instinctual and material needs (Wolfe 2010, xiv). Whereas the initial idea is to extend concerns beyond the human, the way this has often been adopted in IR is through the implicit inversion of this logic. To justify various agendas of environmental politics by arguing that human wellbeing depends on it, given our permeability to an increasingly toxic and dangerous environment, is not a posthuman argument, but a humanist one. In this sense, more-than-human approaches aspiring the posthuman need to be distinguished carefully on the basis of differing motivations as to why we care in the first place.[10] Comparing this approach with other decentring and posthuman tendencies, then IR's more-than-human adaptations are neither strictly posthuman nor do they describe a species or ecological egalitarianism as such, but develop a rationale whereby the human

How I Learned to Stop Worrying and Love Determinism' (2013).

[9]   See for example Cudworth and Hobden (2011).

[10]   See Audra Mitchell's (2014) initial assessment of different types of more-than-human and only human motivations.

existence is protected. This creates an altogether new and peculiar kind of 'liberal' humanism that highlights interdependence, connectedness and mutual vulnerability.

Things and Stuff: Object Oriented Ontology

Trying to think as objects, how they relate to each other and imagining the world from the view point of objects is fundamental to the development of a post-anthropocentric thought. Ensuing from the criticism on the persistence of humanism and the human subject (even if hybridised and pluralised) we see the movement of object oriented philosophy emerging (or OOO). Prominent scholars in this field are, for example, Graham Harman (2003), Levi Bryant (2011) and Ian Bogost (2012) who address precisely the continuation of the subject-object division in the previous attempts of overcoming humanist biases. In general, the OOO proposition is that we need to stop trying to understand the world in terms of subject-object relations. In this sense, rather than analysing phenomena in this dynamic – between the human and environment, human and animal or human and technology – perhaps the things going on independently of that, meaning the action of and between objects, are much more interesting and revealing. Disrupting this dynamic also means that it is no longer the conscious human subject that accesses the world through sensual perception and makes sense of it with its rational mind. Out of the various 'other'-human scholarship OOO has been of particular importance in posthuman debates in IR; a substantial amount of literature takes inspiration from this philosophical tradition focusing on agentic structures and objects by analysing the flows of commodities, weapons, illicit drugs or the lively aspects of borders, passports, printers and so on.[11] To argue that this standpoint seeks a posthuman condition as such seems far-stretched, given that it is primarily concerned with displacing human experience from the centre of IR and security, but remains largely silent over matters of alternatives to the (form of) existence of human beings.

Ultimately, analysing and situating the six variants on the spectrum of posthuman-ness calls into question whether posthuman IR is actually posthuman as none of IR's posthumanesque disquisitions develop an ontology of the international that is based on a form of life that is distinctly and clearly posthuman. Thus, the current state of posthuman IR and security is better described as that of different, less-anthropocentric world views, many of which do not speak to each other because they are in fact emerging from different ontological premises. Rather than being able to escape the all-

---

[11]   See for example Mike Bourne (2012), Kathy Ferguson (2014) and Mark Salter (2012).

too-human focus of IR, the different posthuman efforts rearticulate humanism in a way that is contemporary, more egalitarian, inclusive, less dogmatic and worldly. In short, it can be argued that IR's current posthuman touch is only a neo-humanist modification rather than a posthuman position.

References

Althusser, Louis. 1976. *Essays in Self-Criticism*. London: New Left Books.

Althusser, Louis. 2003. *The Humanist Controversy and Other Writings*, in François Matheron, ed. London and New York: Verso.

Althusser, Louis .2005. *For Marx*. London and New York: Verso.

Badmington, Neil. 2004. *Alien Chic: Posthumanism and the Other Within*. London and New York: Routledge.

Batra, Anupa. 2010. *Experience, Time and the Subject: Deleuze's Transformation of Kant's Critical Philosophy*. Southern Illinois University, PhD.

Bennett, Jane. 2010. *Vibrant Matter: A Political Ecology of Things*. Durham and London: Duke University Press.

Bogost, Ian. 2012. *Alien Phenomenology, or What It's Like to Be a Thing*. Minneapolis: University of Minnesota Press.

Bourne, Michael. 2012. *Security with Things: The Political Materialities and Mobilities of the "Objects" of Security*. Paper presented at the Annual Millennium Conference. 22-23 October 2012. London.

Braidotti, Rosi .2002. *Metamorphoses: Towards a Materialist Theory of Becoming*. Oxford: Oxford UP.

Braidotti, Rosi. 2013. *The Posthuman*. Cambridge: Polity.

Bryant, Levi. 2010. Promises of Posthumanism *Larval Subject* [online]. Available at: http://larvalsubjects.wordpress.com/2010/05/29/promises-of-posthumanism/ [Accessed 25 May 2014].

Bryant, Levi .2011. *The Democracy of Objects*. Ann Arbor: University of Michigan Library.

Butler, Judith .1993. *Bodies That Matter: On the Discursive Limits of Sex*. London: Routledge.

Connolly, William .2011. *A World of Becoming*. Durham and London: Duke UP.

Coole, Diana and Samantha Frost. 2010. *New Materialism: Ontology, Agency, and Politics*. Durham and London: Duke UP.

Cudworth, Erika and Stephen Hobden. 2011. *Posthuman International Relations: Complexity, Ecologism and Global Politics*. London: Zed Books.

Cudworth, Erika and Stephen Hobden. 2013. "Of Parts and Wholes: International Relations Beyond the Human" *Millennium* 41(3): 430-450.

DeLanda, Manuel (1992) *Nonorganic Life*. In Jonathan Crary and Sanford Kwinter, eds. *Zone 6: Incorporations*. New York: Urzone, 129-67.

DeLanda, Manuel (1997) *A Thousand Years of Nonlinear History*. New York: Zone Books.

DeLanda, Manuel (2002) *Intensive Science and Virtual Philosophy*. New York: Continuum.

Deleuze, Gilles. 2001. *Pure Immanence: Essays on A Life*. Trans. Anne Boyman. New York: Zone Books.

Deleuze, Gilles. 2004. *Difference and Repetition*. London: Continuum.

Foucault, Michel. 2005. *The Order of Things*. London: Routledge.

Ferguson, Kathy. 2014. "Anarchist Printers and Presses: Material Circuits of Politics". *Political Theory* 42(4): 391-414.

Haraway, Donna. 1991. *Simians, Cyborgs and Women: The Reinvention of Nature*. New York: Routledge.

Harman, Graham (2003) *Guerrilla Metaphysics: Phenomenology and the Carpentry of Things.* Chicago: Open Court.

Lundborg, Tom and Nick Vaughan-Williams, N. 2015. "New Materialism, Discourse Analysis, and International Relations: A Radical Intertextual Approach" *Review of International Studies*, 41(1): 3-25.

McCarthy, Daniel. 2013. "Technology and 'the International' or: How I Learned to Stop Worrying and Love Determinism" *Millennium: Journal of International Studies* 41(3): 470-490.

Mitchell, Audra. 2014. "Only Human: A Worldly Approach to Security" *Security Dialogue*, 45(1): 5-21.

Moulard-Leonard, Valentine. 2008. *Bergson-Deleuze Encounters: Transcendental Experience and the Thought of the Virtual.* New York: SUNY.

Rutsky, R.L. (2007) "Mutation, History, and Fantasy in the Posthuman" *Subject Matters*, 3(2): 99-112.

Salter, Mark. 2012. *Thing-Power-Politics: Reassembling the Global through the Passport.* Paper presented at the Annual Millennium Conference. 22-23 October 2012. London.

Wolfe, Cary. 2010. *What is Posthumanism?* Minneapolis and London: University of Minnesota Press.

3

Hybridity and Humility: What of the Human in Posthuman Security?

ELKE SCHWARZ

Thinking about 'posthuman security' is no easy task. To begin with, it requires a clear notion of what we mean by 'posthuman'. There are various projects underway to understand what this term can or should signal, and what it ought to comprise. To bring a broadened understanding of 'security' into the mix complicates matters further. In this essay, I argue that a focus on the relation of the human to new technologies of war and security provides one way in which IR can fruitfully engage with contemporary ideas of posthumanism.

For Audra Mitchell (2014) and others, 'posthuman security' serves as a broad umbrella term, under which various non-anthropocentric approaches to thinking about security can be gathered. Rather than viewing security as a purely human good or enterprise, 'posthuman' thinking instead stresses the cornucopia of non-human and technological entities that shape our political ecology, and, in turn, condition our notions of security and ethics. For Mitchell (2014), this process comprises machines, ecosystems, networks, non-human animals, and 'complex assemblages thereof'. Sounds clear enough, but this is where things begin to get complicated.

First, what exactly is 'post' about the posthuman? Often lumped in together under the category of 'posthumanism' are ideas of transhumanism, anti-humanism, post-anthropocentrism, and speculative posthumanism (see for instance David Roden 2015).[12] Each variant has different implications for how

---

[12]   Roden engages with the various discourses on 'posthumanism' today, going to

we think 'security' and 'ethics' after, or indeed beyond, the human. Furthermore, one must ask whether it is even possible to use concepts of security, ethics, and politics after, or beyond the human. These concepts are not only deeply entwined with social constructs; they are also fundamentally *human* constructs. To think 'after-the-human' may well then render 'security' or 'ethics' as concepts entirely obsolete, or at the very least deprive them of a clear referent. And as if this was not enough to wrap one's head around, we further may need to clarify whether it is post-humanity or post-humanness we aim to understand when we strive to think beyond the human. It appears, then, that the posthuman turn in security studies risks raising more questions than it helps to answer at this stage. A clarification of how these terms are used in the literature is thus necessary.

To date, the most clearly defined strands of posthumanist discourse are 'critical posthumanism' and 'transhumanism', as elaborated in the work of Donna Haraway, Neil Badmington, Ray Kurzweil, and Nick Bostrom, among others. Both discourses, although very different in their approach and focus, posit a distinctly modern transformation through which human life has become more deeply enmeshed in science and technology than ever before. In this biologically informed techno-scientific context, human and machine have become isomorphic. The two are fused in both functional and philosophical terms, with technologies shaping human subjectivity as much as human subjectivities shape technology. The question of technology has thus, as Arthur Kroker (2014) puts it, become a question of the human. The question of the human, however, looks decidedly different when viewed through modern techno-scientific logics of functionality and performance. From this perspective, which promotes homogeneity, reproduction, replacement and prophylaxis as a means for the 'technological purification of bodies,' the human appears in ever more degraded terms, as a failure to live up to the promises of technology itself (Baudrillard 1993, 68). The greater the technological augmentation and alterations of life, and the more we invest in technological prostheses and substitutes for it, the greater becomes the necessity for humans to submit to the superiority of the artificial proxy, which carries within it a technologically informed ordering principle that remakes society in its own image. Thus, as contemporary life becomes ever more digitally mediated and technologically enhanced, the human appears more and more as a weak link in the human-machine chain – inadequate at best, 'an infantile malady of a technological apparatus' at worst (Baudrillard 2016, 20).

---

great lengths to highlight the differences between various kinds of ideas that are attached to the term. While these are relevant in the wider context of this article, I lack the space to engage with them in full here.

The interplay between man and machine has, of course, a long-standing history that can easily be conceived of in posthuman terms. This history suggests, in contrast to the rash of hysteric pronouncements about the novelty of our times, that we have *always already* been technologically enhanced and conditioned. I would concur with this point, but see it as doing little to undermine the importance of thinking the human-machine question anew, especially in light of the rapid proliferation and deployment of new technologies related to the waging of wars and the ordering and securing of populations and bodies. In such a context, it is necessary to identify and indeed challenge our submission to technological authority in social and political domains. If we take seriously that new technologies (as artefacts and practices) constitute 'hegemonic political values and beliefs' (Ansorge 2016, 14), then we ought to first question the rationales that are given for such technologies. In particular, we must puncture the pervasive ideology of progress, which says that these new technologies are simply a motor behind the movement toward ever-greater levels of autonomy and artificial intelligence. The rapid movement towards greater autonomy in military affairs itself entails another process, which is the reconfiguration of new machine-humans for a transformed ethos for the administration of war. It is therefore crucial, at least from a critical perspective, to get a handle on the kind of machine-human subjectivities our new ways of war and security are producing.

In a fervent drive for progress, scientists and roboticists work feverishly to replace what we hitherto have known and understood as human life with bigger, better, bolder robot versions of what life ought to be – fully acknowledging, if not embracing, the possibility of rendering humans increasingly obsolete. Machines are designed to outpace human capabilities, while old-fashioned human organisms cannot progress at an equal rate and will, eventually, 'clearly face extinction' (Singer 2009, 415). Fears about this trajectory are being voiced by elites and experts of all stripes. Technology tycoon Elon Musk, for example, has recently issued a dire warning about the dangers of rapidly advancing Artificial Intelligence (AI) and the prospects of killer robots capable of 'deleting humans like spam' (in Anderson 2014). Musk is not alone in his cautious assessment. Nick Bostrom (2015), in a recent UN briefing, echoes such sentiments when he warns that AI may well pose the greatest existential risk to humanity today, if current developments are any indication of what is likely to come in the future. A group of 3037 AI/Robotics researchers has signed an open letter calling for a ban of autonomous weapons. The letter was signed by a further 17376 endorsers, among them Stephen Hawking, Elon Musk, Steve Wozniak and Daniel C. Dennett. Other science and technology icons, like Bill Gates, have joined the chorus too, seeing new combinations of AI and advanced robotics as a grave source of insecurity going forward.

Statements like these betray not only a certain fatalism on the part of humans who have, in fact, invented, designed, and realised said autonomous machines; they also pose the question of whether the advancement of technology can indeed still be considered a human activity, or whether technology itself has moved into a sphere beyond human control and comprehension. Humans, as conceived by transhumanist discourses, are involved in a conscious process of perpetually overcoming themselves through technology. For transhumanists, the human is 'a work-in-progress,' perpetually striving toward perfection in a process of techno-scientifically facilitated evolution that promises to leave behind the 'half-baked beginning[s]' of contemporary humanity (Bostrom 2005, 4). Transhumanism, however, is – as David Roden (2015, 13-14) points out – underwritten by a drive to improve and better human life. It is, he notes, a fundamentally normative position, whereby the freedom to self-design through technology is affirmed as an extension of human freedom. Transhumanism 'is thus an ethical claim to the effect that technological enhancement of human capacities is a desirable aim' (Roden 2015, 9). However, the pursuit of transhumanism through AI, the 'NBIC' suite of technologies (which comprises of nanotechnology, biotechnology, information technology and the cognitive sciences), or networked computing technologies more generally does not guarantee a privileged place for humans in the historical future. Rather, the ongoing metamorphosis of human and machine threatens 'an explosion of artificial intelligence that would leave humans cognitively redundant' (Roden 2015, 21). In such a scenario, the normative position of transhumanism necessarily collapses into a speculative view on the posthuman, wherein both the shape of the historical future and the place of the human within this become an open question. Indeed, in the future world there may be no place for the human at all.

This perhaps unintended move toward a speculative technological future harbours a paradox. First, the conception of science and technology as improving or outmoding the human is an inherently human construct and project – it is neither determined nor initiated by a non-human entity which demands or elicits submission based on their philosophical autonomy; rather, it is through human thought and imagination that this context emerges in the first place. The human is thus always already somehow immanent in the technological post-human. Yet at the same time, it is the overcoming, at the risk outmoding, human cognition and functionality that forms the basic wager of speculative posthumanism.[13] Thus, while the posthuman future will be a

---

[13] At this point we can clarify the differences between humanism, transhumanism, posthumanism, and the posthuman. By 'humanism' I mean those discourses and projects that take some fixed idea of the human as their natural centre, and by 'transhumanism' I mean those that grapple with or aim at an active technical alteration of the human as such. I reserve the term 'posthumanism' for those discourses that seek

product of human enterprise, it will also be a future in which the unaugmented human appears more and more as flawed, error-prone, and fallible. Contemporary techno-enthusiasm therefore carries within it the seeds of our anxiety, shame, and potential obsolescence as 'mere humans'.

This new hierarchical positioning of the human vis-à-vis technology represents a shift in both. Put simply, the 'creator' of machines accepts a position of inferiority in relation to his or her creations (be these robots, cyborgs, bionic limbs, health apps, or GPS systems, to give just a few examples). This surrender relies on an assumed techno-authority of produced 'life' on the one hand, and an acceptance of inferiority – as an excess of the human's desire to 'surpass man', to become machine – on the other. The inherently fallible and flawed human can never fully-meet the standards of functionality and perfection that are the mandate for the machines they create. And it is precisely within this hybridity of being deity (producer) and mortal (un-produced human) that an unresolved tension resides. Heidegger's student and Hannah Arendt's first husband, Günther Anders, has given much thought to this. His work extensively grapples with the condition that characterises the switch from *creator* to *creatum,* and he diagnoses this distinctly modern condition as one of 'Promethean Shame.' It is the very technologisation of our being that gives rise to this shame, which implies a shamefulness about not-being-machine, encapsulating both awe at the superior qualities of machine existence, and admiration for the flawless perfection with which machines promise to perform specific roles or tasks. In this distinctly modern condition, human worth and moral standards are measured against the parameters of rational and flawlessly functioning machines, producing a normed environment in which the human cannot fully fit in. To overcome this shame, Anders argues, humans began to enhance their biological capacities, striving to make themselves more and more like machines.

The concept of shame is significant not simply as 'overt shame' – which is akin to a 'feeling experienced by a child when it is in some way humiliated by another person' (Giddens 2003, 65) – but also as an instantiation of being exposed as insufficient, flawed, or erroneous. This latter form of shame is concerned with 'the body in relation to the mechanisms of self-identity' (Giddens 2003, 67), and is intrinsically bound up with the modern human-technology complex. To compensate, adapt to, and fit into a technologized environment, humans seek to become machines through technological enhancement, not merely to better themselves, but also to meet the quasi-

---

to think a future in which the technical alteration of the human has given rise to new forms of life that can no longer properly be called human. The 'posthuman' is a name for these new, unknown forms of life.

moral mandate of becoming a rational and progressive product: ever-better, ever-faster, ever-smarter, superseding the limited corporeality of the human, and eventually the human self. This mandate clearly adheres to a capitalist logic, shaping subjectivities in line with a drive toward expansion and productivity. It is, however, a fundamentally technological drive insofar as functionality per se, rather than expansion or productivity, is the measure of all. Nowhere is this more starkly exemplified than in current relations between human soldiers and unmanned military technology.

Consider, for example, military roboticist Ronald Arkin's conviction that the human is the weakest link in the kill chain. Such a logos – which is derived from the efficient and functional character as technology as such – suggests that the messy problems of war and conflict can be worked away through the abstract reasoning of machines. Arkin (2015), one of the most vocal advocates of producing 'ethical' lethal robots by introducing an 'ethical governor' into the technology, inadvertently encapsulates both aspects of techno-authority perfectly when he asks: 'Is it not our responsibility as scientists to look for effective ways to reduce man's inhumanity to man through technology?' For Arkin, the lethal robot is able to make a more ethical decision than the human, simply by being programmed to a use a pathway for decision-making based on abstracted laws of war and armed conflict. The human, in her flawed physiological and mental capacity, is thus to be governed by the (at least potential) perfection of a machine authority.

This is by no means a mere brainchild of outsider techno-enthusiasm – quite the contrary: the US Department of Defense (DoD) is an active solicitor of increasingly intelligent machines that, one day soon, will be able to 'select and engage targets without further intervention by a human operator,' and will possess the reasoning capacity needed to 'assess situations and make recommendations or decisions,' including, most likely, kill decisions (Zacharias 2015). Consider, for example, the DoD Autonomy Roadmap, presented in March 2015, which sets out the agenda for greater levels of machine intelligence and learning (MPRI), as well as rational goals for human-machine interactions and collaboration (HASIC), and a concept of 'Calibrated Trust' intended to create for the human an understanding of 'what the [machine] agent is doing and why' (Bornstein 2015). With the drive for greater technology autonomy comes the apparent desire for greater technology authority. 'Human-autonomy teaming' is a partnership in which the human, at least ostensibly, still decides when and how to invoke technology's autonomy (Endsley 2015). Whether this is possible or even realistic in contexts, such as those where humans lack the sensory capabilities or computing powers required for the task they are undertaking, is very much a question that needs asking. Particularly as on a not-too-distant horizon looms the spectre of intelligent machine autonomy, equipped with superior sensors, agility, and reasoning capacities. The hierarchies of authority over the most morally challenging of decisions, such as killing in war, are likely to experience a shift overall toward a pure techno-logos.

Leaving the heated debate about Lethal Autonomous Weapons Systems (LAWS) – or Killer Robots – aside for a moment, this logic is testament to the Promethean Shame identified by Anders half a century prior. In his writings, Anders astutely realised the ethical implications of such a shift in hierarchical standing. As Christopher Müller notes in his discussion of Anders' work, the contemporary world is one in which machines are 'taking care' of both functional problems as well as fundamentally existential questions; '[i]t is hence the motive connotations of taking care to relieve of worry, responsibility and moral effort that are of significance here' (Müller 2015). It is in such a shift toward a techno-authority that ethical responsibility is removed from the human realm and conceived of instead in techno-scientific terms. Ethics as a technical matter 'mimes scientific analysis; both are based on sound facts and hypothesis testing; both are technical practices' (Haraway 1997, 109). Arkin's argument for the inclusion of an ethics component in military robots is paradigmatic. In his understanding of ethics, Arkin (2015) frames the logical coding of robotic machines as ethically superior to the human – indeed, he calls the module an 'ethical governor.' The rationale underpinning this position takes for granted a number of things. One is that the human can, and indeed must, be measured against the technology to assess her functional performance. Another is that the characteristics of those who pose a risk to security can clearly be ascertained and acted on within this techno-logos.

And finally, it is assumed that this reasoning is rational and consistent and therefore moral. Together these turn ethics into a task of identifying and eliminating persons of risk as humanely as possible, and with as few people's lives on the line as technology can permit. The underlying question, then, shifts from whether it is ethical to kill, to whether technological systems would do the killing better than humans. If it has been determined by algorithmic calculation, for example, that all military-aged males in a certain geographic region, displaying certain suspicious patterns of life behaviour, pose a potential security risk, then the ethical task at hand is to kill better and more humanely. The 'ethical' dimension of a kill decision is thereby engineered into a technological system, so that the actual moment of a real ethical decision is always already pre-empted and thereby eliminated. Where ethics is abstracted and coded, it leaves us with little possibility to challenge the ethicality of the context within which the ethical programme unfolds. And where ethics is coded, it curbs the ethical responsibility of the individual subject. I address this problem of a scientifically informed rationale of ethics as a matter of technology elsewhere (see for instance Schwarz 2015). What I would like to stress here, though, are the possible futures associated with this trajectory.

The speculative nature of posthumanism requires that we creatively imagine how traditional concepts of humanity, such as ethics or security, might comprehensively be affected and altered by technology. In other words, the rise (and fall) of homo technologicus requires that we address the question concerning technology imaginatively. A challenge in modern thinking about technology was and still is the apparent gap between the technologies we produce and our imagination regarding the uses to which this technology is put. Here, I return to Günther Anders. For Anders (1972), this is a gap between product and mind, between the production (*Herstellung*) of technology and our imagination (*Vorstellung*) regarding the consequences of its use. Letting this gap go unaddressed produces space for a technological authority to emerge, wherein ethical questions are cast in increasingly technical terms. This has potentially devastating implications for ethics as such. As Anders notes, the discrepancy between *Herstellung* and *Vorstellung* signifies that we no longer know what we do. This, in turn, takes us to the very limits of our responsibility, for 'to "assume responsibility" is nothing other than to admit to one's deed, the effects of which one had conceived (*vorgestellt*) in advance' (Anders 1972, 73-74). And what becomes of ethics, when we can no longer claim any responsibility?

References

Anders, Günther. 1972. *Endzeit und Zeitende*. München: C.H. Beck.

Anderson, Lessley. 2014. "Elon Musk: A Machine Tasked with Getting Rid of Spam Could End Humanity" *Vanity Fair.* Online at: http://www.vanityfair.com/news/tech/2014/10/elon-musk-artificial-intelligence-fear/ [Accessed 15 November 2016]

Ansorge, Josef. 2016. *Identify and Sort: How Digital Power Changed World Politics*. London: C. Hurst and Co. Ltd.

Arkin, Ronald. 2015. "Lethal Autonomous Weapons Systems and the Plight of the Noncombatant", Presentation to the CCW Meeting of Experts on Lethal Autonomous Weapons in Geneva, 13-16 May 2015. Online at: http://www.unog.ch/80256EDD006B8954/(httpAssets)/FD01CB0025020DDFC1257CD70060EA38/$file/Arkin_LAWS_technical_2014.pdf/ [Accessed 23 November 2015]

Baudrillard, Jean. 2016. *Why Hasn't Everything Already Disappeared?* Translated by Chris Turner. London: Seagull Books.

Baudrillard, Jean. 1993. *The Transparency of Evil: Essays on Extreme Phenomena*. Translated by James Benedict. London: Verso.

Bornstein, Jon. 2015. "US Department of Defense Autonomy Roadmap: Autonomy Community of Interest", presented to the NDIA Annual Science and Engineering Technology Conference, 24-26 March 2015. Online at: http://www.defenseinnovationmarketplace.mil/resources/AutonomyCOI_NDIA_Briefing20150319.pdf [Accessed 6 January 2017].

Bostrom, Nick. 2015. "Briefing on Existential Risk for the UN Interregional Crime and Justice Research Institute," 7 October 2015. Online at: http://webtv.un.org/watch/chemical-biological-radiological-and-nuclear-cbrn-national-action-plans-rising-to-the-challenges-of-international-security-and-the-emergence-of-artificial-intelligence/4542739995001 [Accessed 04 January 2017].

Bostrom, Nick. 2005. "Transhumanist Values." *Journal of Philosophical Research* 30 (Supplement): 3-14.

Endsley, Mica R. 2015. "Autonomous Horizons: Systems Autonomy in the Air Force – A Path to the Future," United States Air Force Office of the Chief Scientist, AF/ST TR 15-01, June 2015. Online at: http://www.af.mil/Portals/1/documents/SECAF/AutonomousHorizons.pdf?timestamp=1435068339702/ [Accessed 25 November 2015]

Giddens, Anthony. 2013. *Modernity and Self-Identity: Self and Society in the Late Modern Age*. Cambridge: Polity.

Haraway, Donna. 1997. *Modest_Witness@Second_Millennium. FemaleMan©_Meets_OncoMouse™*. London: Routledge.

Kroker, Arthur. 2014. *Exits to the Posthuman Future*. Cambridge: Polity.

Mitchell, Audra. 2016. "Dispatches from the Robot Wars; Or, What is Posthuman Security?" *The Disorder of Things*, 27 July 2014. Online at: http://thedisorderofthings.com/2014/07/24/dispatches-from-the-robot-wars-or-what-is-posthuman-security/ [Accessed 15 November 2016.]

Müller, Christopher. 2015."We are Born Obsolete: Günther Anders's (Post) humanism", *Critical Posthumanism* [Website], January 2015. Online at: http:// criticalposthumanism.net/?page_id=433/ [Accessed 15 November 2016]

Roden, David. 2015. *Posthuman Life: Philosophy at the Edge of the Human.* Abingdon: Routledge.

Schwarz, Elke. 2015. "Prescription Drones: On the Techno-Biopolitical Regimes of Contemporary 'Ethical Killing'", *Security Dialogue* 41 (1): 59-75.

Singer, Peter. 2009. *Wired for War: The Robotics Revolution and Conflict in the 21st Century.* London: Penguin.

Zacharias, Greg. 2015. "Advancing the Science and Acceptance of Autonomy for Future Defense Systems" Presentation to the House Armed Services Subcommittee Hearing on Emerging Threats and Capabilities, 19 November 2015. Online at: http://www.airforcemag.com/testimony/Documents/2015/ November 2015/111915zacharias.pdf/ [Accessed 15 November 2016]

4

Anthropocentrism and the Politics of the Living

RAFI YOUATT

The 'end of nature' has been widely proclaimed. At one level, it refers to the ongoing biophysical destruction of ecosystems, habitats, forests, species, individual creatures, and climate through widely varying processes of extraction, consumption, and production. But at another level, it also references the end of a particularly western idea of nature, as something external to human politics, economy, and culture (Latour 2004). Such an idea of nature, in which the non-human world was largely taken as a form of 'standing reserve' for state extraction (Smith 2009), was central to the development of the contemporary state system under which the first, material end of nature proceeded, undergirding projects of colonialism and capitalism.

In this context, the long, slow crisis of biodiversity loss marks a double end of nature. The daily extinction of species, the general homogenization of species around the world, and the transformation of terrestrial and marine ecosystems, all due to human activity, all point to an end of material nature. Biodiversity loss, along with climate change, thus form some of the key conditions for the so-called Anthropocene – an era marked by deep human intervention into the deepest processes of nature. Nature, if it ever was external, is no longer so, and neither political practice nor political thought can rely on it quite so easily.

One reading of the relative lack of scientific knowledge about most species, and the general lack of world political attention paid to this crisis, is that nature is being extinguished before humans even know about it.[14] Moreover,

---

[14]   Thanks are due to the participants in the Global Politics without Ignorance Workshop, held in October 2016 at the New School for Social Research. The discussion there informs a number of points in this article.

even if we were to know more, we might not care. But this reading, while true in one sense, is also misleading. Non-human life has in many ways been one of the most intensively studied aspects of various political projects, ranging from colonial preoccupations with biology, species, collection and cataloguing, to the deep forms of knowledge and manipulation generated through contemporary global agricultural practices, to the forms of nature that are being produced in the Anthropocene not by neglect or distance but by deep, thorough-going intervention in nature. So a tempting way to think anthropocentrism and global politics – as a full, wilful blindness about non-human life – doesn't seem to be entirely right.

And yet, as Audra Mitchell (2016a) contends, not only is there an enormous blind spot about biodiversity loss, in the sense of political awareness about extinction, but this blind spot is produced through structural conditions of knowledge production. This is not just the natural sciences failing to complete their cumulative processes of collecting information, but also social sciences, including IR, failing to contemplate the challenges of planet politics (Burke et al. 2016). There are also blind spots when it comes to the ways in which we think about international politics and non-human life and persons, and in particular around the question of who or what can be seen as a political actor. Central to this blind spot are formations of *anthropocentrism.*

Anthropocentrism is a difficult term, given that it is not always entirely clear what constitutes the 'anthropos' or 'the human', nor is it clear what it means for such an entity to be 'centred'. I use it as a rather large term to cover a range of perspectives that in some way trouble the exclusive centrality of the human to our concepts and analyses of political life, *and* call into question that category of the human itself, prompting us to ask about multiple versions of the human articulated in and with different assemblages of the non-human, including animal, natural, material, and technological. Specifically, multispecies and multi-being assemblages, I suggest by the end of the article, may be a more fundamental political unit of global politics than we have previously tended to assume in IR.

There are also blind spots in anti-anthropocentric thought, when it comes to their own conception of the human, who sometimes paradoxically re-emerges as a universal figure, defined by species rather than history, carrying moral capacities to order and re-order the world. At the 'end of nature,' such a version of the human is regularly being articulated in global environmental discourses, such as climate change and Anthropocene, which in many ways *do* aim to reorient our understandings of what international relations is for. Such claims miss the historical responsibility of some humans over others;

they underrate the specific structuring forces of colonialisms, capitalisms, and geopolitics, rather than species activity; and the historical and cultural human, rather than the biological human.

This article first suggests that any significant evaluation of anthropocentrism requires a critical engagement with the anthropos, or the human that is presumed to be at the centre of anthropocentrism, and it requires engagements with the specific ways that nonhuman life figures in these productions as well as on their own terms. The second part of the article suggests some of the pathways that such an analysis opens for IR, engaging both with interspecies relations and logics, and with the politics of collective personhood.

Anthropocentrism

What I want to do first is to map some of the critiques that work around anthropocentrism, and then move to an analysis of the important problematics that they open up for global politics. One general way that anthropocentrism is approached in global politics is as a matter of moral or ethical privileging of the human, as more important than various figurations of non-humans – whether nature or nonhuman animals.[15] Here, the critique is that humans have unfairly, or unwittingly, privileged their moral standing over non-human life, which has been reduced to some form of purely instrumental use. In environmental ethics, then, the response to this kind of anthropocentrism has been to discuss alternative subjects of moral value, such as biocentrism, in which all forms of life share in some form of value, or ecocentrism, putting ecosystems front and centre.

One of the most powerful aspects of this critique has been to show that anthropocentrism is not, as some assert, a problem that is inherent to being human – one is not inherently anthropocentric by being human. Rather, like other systems of moral value, it is possible to imagine other systems of moral value. The downsides, though, are twofold: first, such moves reinscribe the idea of a morally reasoning human subject as the arbiter of value, which seems to come full circle to the very problem it is trying to avoid. It removes us from the pull and push of the places where responses-among-and-between living creatures plays out, or where relations of 'response-ability,' as Haraway (2008) puts it, play out. Second, by staying largely on moral and ethical terrain, it also avoids the difficult questions about how such value systems play out in political practice. While this is not a failing of moral theory, per se, it does limit its utility in aiming to understand contemporary political

---

[15]   These points are explored in greater depth in (Youatt 2014). On ecocentrism and international relations, see the pioneering work of Robyn Eckersley (2004)

ecological formations.

Rather than *moral* valuation then, other work has pushed us significantly to think about the *analysis* of global politics from a less anthropocentric perspective. Here, rather than assuming human beings to be the sole agents and authors of political events – whether as intentional agents, or as the bearers of social structures, social meanings, and discourses – a more careful, non-anthropocentric analysis of political life would reveal those accounts to be fictions that bury many forms of nonhuman agency under ideas like 'unintentional consequences' or 'structural constraint' or, in fact, ignored entirely. Instead, as Timothy Mitchell (2002) puts it in his seminal chapter in *Rule of Experts,* it means making agency a question to be pursued, rather than one to be answered in advance.

This empirical multiplication of political agency, at its best, shows not just a banal sense of causality through non-human materialities that intervene between human agents, but shows instead the specific kinds of differences that non-human entities make in particular political constellations (Robbins 2007; Salter 2015). At times, this work also suggests that greater *analytical* attention to the networks of becoming that make up politics also entails a shift in our *ethical* perspective, or at least an openness to the world that is more likely to result in positive environmental outcomes.

In its stronger guises, an analytical commitment against anthropocentrism involves an *ontological* argument, or a claim for what Jane Bennett (2001, 160-66), following Stephen White, calls 'weak ontology.' Much of Bruno Latour's work (Latour 1993; 2004) also functions in this space – advancing neither a moral claim, per se, nor a political claim about particular assemblages over, against, or with others, but rather a more general ontological claim about the way the world works across the Great Divides of nature, culture, using specific cases as examples.

But there is a missing element in this analytical anti-anthropocentrism when it does not directly call into question the production of the multiple humans in anthropocentrism – that is, in focusing its attention on non-human actants, it sometimes assumes (tacitly, at least) that the 'human' in anthropocentrism is best described as a category encompassing the entire species, rather than asking how particular versions of the human come into being, and what the regimes of inclusion and exclusion are around those figures.[16]

A third engagement with anthropocentrism, then, moves directly into this

---

[16]   Among those who have raised this issue are (Sundberg 2014)

political space, to ask not only about moral questions of valuation, or empirical questions of distributed agency, but a number of political questions about hierarchy. It asks about the making of humanity as a category of practice – across lines of race (Anderson 2013), coloniality (Mavhunga 2011), migrants and borders (Sundberg 2011), war (Kosek 2011), humanitarianism (Ticktin 2011), and commodification (Tsing 2012). Anthropocentrism here is also a historically positioned ideology, working within circuits of colonialism, liberalism, and capitalism, but it works unevenly across place, space, and time. It is therefore more accurate to think about anthropocentrisms in the plural.

Seeing anthropocentrisms as political ideologies does not mean solely approaching them through forms of critique. Rather, precisely the terms on which anthropocentrism is constituted – on human language and reason as the grounds of political belonging, for example – mask the many ways that 'non-linguistic' activity *already* constitutes the political. This means a turn *back* to the areas on which the human is constituted – and here, it is useful to return to some of the moral and ontological critiques of humanism, but with a more political eye. For example, the divide between human and animal comes into view not just as one separating humans from non-human animals, but as a more general category of animality that structures life conditions for a range of creatures. It also means that a more thorough reading of the political, through non-anthropocentric lenses, means asking more fully about the ways we interact with non-human life as itself political – across the wide range of contexts in which that happens – and as worthy of our attention.

So anthropocentrism in this particular sense – as a question of political ontology and historically positioned productions of differences in and across species lines – opens up a very fertile and important set of issues in global politics. Rather than looking at environmental issues solely as matters for human politics to sort out, for example, it asks us to look at intersections between them and the production of hierarchy through shifting categories of species, animal, living, and natural and through interactive practices among humans and other species. Rather than looking at questions around non-human animals as a question of how far existing rights should be extended, it asks us to think about how concepts of animality function to structure the lives of both human and non-human lives. And rather than looking to move past the human or to transcend the human, it asks us to stay with the production of different kinds of humans as a question of political analysis.[17]

---

[17]   In many ways, this approach is not new – though it has been largely absent from Euro-American international relations. This work comes from anthropology, geography, political ecology, science studies, and elsewhere.

Politics of the Living?

On one hand, I am particularly committed to understanding a politics of the living, moving slightly away from the analytic space of new materialisms. When materialisms become political, they often seem to reduce to a kind of weak anthropocentrism, where people are walking assemblages, and we care about the assemblages because we care about the people. But there is something important in the combination of a) the squishy, embodied fact of living bodies (Calarco 2008; Hayles 1999), and b) in particular about the interpretive moments that living beings share (Kohn 2013; Uexkull 1982), and c) the ways they increasingly seem to me to be enmeshed in a kind of biopolitics of the living, one that is both problematic in its effects, but promising in the resistant alliances it points to (Youatt 2008), and d) offers a potential for particular interspecies assemblages as politically salient (Tsing 2012).

We could take this to be an opportunity to start to enquire about how particular *productions* of humanism work within a broader politics, practice, and symbolic economy of life. To take one example, at the US-Mexico border, I have been trying to understand the circulation of anthropocentrism, across species lines, and how this implies a sense of the political as something already involving multiple species – not in a benign sense of inclusion, but as a sometimes violent, exclusionary process that works alongside possibilities of affiliation, and companion species. Who counts as human, subhuman, animal, endangered, protected, and when? Ocelot politics involve an assemblage of endangerment: an endangered species in the US under the endangered species act (though ocelots fare much better in Central and South America), and discourses around endangered nation and culture; and endangerment that ocelots face trying to cross roads (the major source of death for ocelots in the region). Invasiveness, too, is a multispecies assemblage at the border: the invasive Nilgai antelope (brought from India to Texas for hunting purposes in the 1930s, and now largely feral), crossing into Mexico, and re-crossing a quarantine line designed to keep ticks bearing cattle fever out of American rangelands. This quarantine line runs parallel to the border, now with designed tactical infrastructure (the product of a limited wall-building project) designed to keep illegal immigrants out, or at least minimised. Invasiveness and endangerment, central to IR imaginaries around security, might be in this case best understood not as a discourse, nor as security facts, but as a multi-species and multi-practice assemblage.

What does it mean to elevate certain species over others, and sometimes for them to be elevated above other humans? In the most challenging vein of inquiry, what would it mean to start to think about politics as something multiple communities of different species engage in – how does one research something like that as a matter of global politics? (In one sense, we already do, in any research involving claims about eco-systems, which are made up of living species interacting with one another, on and through various non-living elements; why ecosystems and their constituent parts should remain off limits to IR is a mystery, given that this has been taken up by anthropologists, environmental studies, geographers, and others).

On the other hand, the analytics of new materialism have opened up the question of how apparently non-living, or abiotic things like mountains, canyons, buildings, IEDs and deserts, act on us, interact with, disrupt and make possible political life (Boyce 2015; Grove 2016; Salter 2015). But I am increasingly cognizant that my relationship with the non-living comes out of a particular kind of philosophy of life and nature (rooted in biological sciences), and a particular politics as well (secular). In my more recent research, I have become interested in how apparently non-living things, like mountains or ecosystems, are encountered by global governance, and what it means for them to be positioned as non-living. I have been particularly influenced by anthropological work, here including Eduardo Viveiros de Castro (2004), Marisol de la Cadena (2010), and Eduardo Kohn (2013). This body of work pushes hard against my assumptions about the nature of the divide between the living and the non-living – what does it mean for Mt. Taylor in New Mexico to be a living being, for example, as asserted by Zuni tribes (Colwell and Ferguson 2014)?

Recent efforts to use 'sacred mountains' as a new marker for setting areas of international conservation similarly highlight claims about the personhood of mountains. To take on example, Mt. Kailash (or Kangrinboque) in Tibetan China, draws pilgrims from Buddhist, Hindu, Bon (animist), and frequently, syncretic traditions, who come yearly for circumambulation. The site is also beginning to be developed by China and perhaps India and Nepal as a tourist destination, and there is potential for mineral resource extraction nearby. Each of these religious traditions work within worldviews in which Mt. Kailash is not a mountain per se, but a person or divinity who is enmeshed in a wide-ranging set of relations that go beyond its geographic site, including social and ecological relations. While such personhoods are usually relegated to 'religious belief' in secular politics, perhaps such framings are too biological in their limiting of living beings. Rather than resolve the question of what is living and what is not, it might be more important to understand the living in a more open fashion, and as itself a site of political contestation, sometimes in incommensurable ways.

What do we make of multiple personhoods existing in the same place, then?

Can we mix the registers of collective state personhood with collective persons that are perhaps divinities or perhaps invoking nonhuman living beings? What happens when that place is transnational, rather than contained within state frameworks of law? These questions cannot be answered on an intellectual scaffolding that has already determined who gets to count as a collective person up front, nor one that limits discussions of the human to biological registers or to teleological, universalist humanism.[18]

In these examples, the question starts to shift from the ways that forms of life interact with one another against an abiotic backdrop on which varieties of cultural meanings are projected, to one where 'the living' is not yet settled. In this context, we might wish to work through the problems of understanding these other formulations of the living, and at times, we may need to understand that these worldviews are not commensurable with one another – that is, they cannot be fully reduced to one particular framework or fully translated, on any side. At the same time, neither should we assume full incommensurability of worlds, as the very process of interpretation, nor that politics involve forms of learning, understanding, and translation. The question of what is and is not commensurable, and how they are made so, is ultimately a contextual one – it is something that we can ask about in global politics, rather than stipulate up front.

Questions around the interactions, sortings, and practices of living beings to produce international outcomes; questions of who is a person and who is a collective person, and why; and questions about how multiple humanisms work in practice, are key avenues of inquiry that open up in IR around the politics of life after anthropocentrism.

References

Anderson, Kay. 2013. *Race and the Crisis of Humanism*. New York: Routledge.

Boyce, Geoffrey A., 2015. "The Rugged Border: Surveillance, policing and the dynamic materiality of the US/Mexico frontier." *Environment and Planning, D: Society and Space* 34 (2):1-18.

Burke, Anthony, Stefanie Fishel, Audra Mitchell, Simon Dalby, and Daniel J.

---

[18]   Similar questions exist around the emergence of collective persons as legal subjects in what gets translated as "rights for nature" politics, in Ecuador, Bolivia, New Zealand, and a number of other localities. See (Fitz-Henry 2014; Grear 2013; Shelton 2015)

Levine. 2016. "Planet Politics: A Manifesto from the End of IR." *Millennium* 44 (3):499-523.

Cadena, Marisol De La. 2010. "Indigenous Cosmopolitics in the Andes: Conceptual Reflections beyond 'Politics'." *Cultural Anthropology* 25 (2):334-370.

Calarco, Matthew. 2008. *Zoographies: The Question of the Animal from Heidegger to Derrida*. New York: Columbia University Press.

Colwell, Chip, and T.J. Ferguson. 2014. "The Snow-Capped Mountain and the Uranium Mine: Zuni Heritage and the Landscape Scale in Cultural Resource Management." *Advances in Archaeological Practice* 2 (4):234-251.

Eckersley, Robyn. 2004. *The Green State: Rethinking Democracy and Sovereignty*. Cambridge: MIT Press.

Fitz-Henry, Erin. 2014. Decolonising Personhood. In *Wild Law in Practice*, edited by Michelle Maloney and Peter Burdon, 133-148. New York:Routledge.

Grear, Anna. 2013. "Law's Entities: Complexity, Plasticity, and Justice." *Jurisprudence: An International Journal of Legal and Political Thought* 4 (1):76-101.

Grove, Jairus. 2016. "An Insurgency of Things: Foray into the World of Improvised Explosive Devices." *International Political Sociology* 10 (4):1-19.

Haraway, Donna. 2008. *When Species Meet*. Minneapolis: University of Minnesota Press.

Hayles, N. Katherine. 1999. *How We Became Posthuman: Virtual Bodies in Cybernetics, Literature, and Informatics*. Chicago: University of Chicago Press.

Kohn, Eduardo. 2013. *How Forests Think: Toward an Anthropology Beyond the Human*: University of California Press.

Kosek, Jake. 2011. "The Natures of the Beast: On the New Uses of the Honeybee." In *Global Political Ecology*, edited by Richard Peet, Paul Robbins, and Michael Watts. New York: Routledge.

Latour, Bruno. 1993. *We Have Never Been Modern*. Cambridge, Mass.: Harvard University Press.

Latour, Bruno. 2004. *Politics of Nature: How to Bring the Sciences into Democracy*. Cambridge: Harvard University Press.

Mavhunga, Clapperton Chakanetsa. 2011. "Vermin Beings: On Pestiferous Animal and Human Game." *Social Text* 29 (1):151-176.

Mitchell, Audra. 2016a. "Beyond Biodiversity and Species: Problematising Extinction." *Theory, Culture, and Society* 33 (5):23-42.

Mitchell, Audra. 2016b. "Is IR going extinct?" *European Journal of International Relations* 23 (1): 3-25.

Mitchell, Timothy. 2002. *Rule of Experts: Egypt, Techno-Politics, Modernity*. Berkeley: University of California Press.

Robbins, Paul. 2007. *Lawn People: How Grasses, Weeds, and Chemicals Make Us Who We Are*. Philadelphia: Temple University Press.

Salter, Mark, ed. 2015. *Making Things International 1: Circuits and Motion*. Minneapolis: University of Minnesota Press.

Shelton, Dinah. 2015. "Nature as Legal Person." *VertigO: La Revue Électronique en Sciences de l'Environment* Hors-série 22 (September 2015):http://vertigo.revues.org/16188.

Smith, Mick. 2009. "Against Ecological Sovereignty: Agamben, Politics, and Globalization." *Environmental Politics* 18 (1):99-116.

Sundberg, Juanita. 2011. "Diabolic Caminos in the Desert and Cat Fights on the Río: A Posthumanist Political Ecology of Boundary Enforcement in the United States–Mexico Borderlands " *Annals of the Association of American Geographers* 101 (2):318-336.

Sundberg, Juanita. 2014. "Decolonising Posthumanist Geographies." *Cultural Geographies* 21 (1):33-47.

Ticktin, Miriam. 2011. *Casualties of Care: Immigration and the Politics of Humanitarianism in France*. Berkeley: University of California Press.

Tsing, Anna. 2012. "Unruly Edges: Mushrooms as Companion Species." *Environmental Humanities* 1 (1):141-154.

Uexkull, Jakob Von. 1982. "The Theory of Meaning." *Semiotica* 42 (1):25-82.

Viveiros De Castro, Eduardo. 2004. "Perspectival Anthropology and the Method of Controlled Equivocation." *Tipiti: Journal of the Society for the Anthropology of Lowland South America* 2 (1):3-22.

Youatt, Rafi. 2008. "Counting Species: Biopower and the Global Biodiversity Census." *Environmental Values* 17 (3):393-417.

Youatt, Rafi. 2014. "Interspecies Relations, International Relations: Rethinking Anthropocentric Politics." *Millennium* 43 (1):207-223.

5

Performing the Posthuman: An Essay in Three Acts

STEFANIE FISHEL

Setting the Scene

The posthuman is defined by its conceptual complexity. It is not quite a temporal creation of what will come after the human, but is often thought of in the future tense. What will *homo sapiens* become *next*? Alternatively, the posthuman, like postmodernity, often overlaps with the modern and the pre-modern. The posthuman can be located in the ethical writings of Spinoza (Braidotti 2013), Thomas Hobbes' Leviathan (Shapin and Schaffer 1985), and Mary Shelley's Creature (Carretero-Gonzalez 2016). The posthuman can be the 'more-than-human' (Massumi 2014) or an ethical understanding of a subject that can traverse worlds, both human and nonhuman (Braidotti 2013; Mitchell 2014).

In theorising the posthuman, we return to the world of the nonhuman animal or rethink biopolitics writ large as a 'displacement of the subject' (Parikka 2015). Thinking the posthuman is part of a tradition that knows that any theories of subjectivity must include the embodied nature of what we then name 'subjects' (Braidotti 2006). It questions the divisions we have created between these subjects and objects, the human and animal. While it is not always a biological entity or an evolution of the human animal, it is entangled with both natural and technological systems. As a cyborg, the posthuman can redefine our relationship to nature (Haraway 1991) or be the sum of human fears that our technology will overcome and control us.[19] The Terminator is at

---

[19] I leave aside transhumanism in this chapter as it takes a fundamentally different approach to technology and the human body. See Hayles (1999) for a history of cybernetics and bodies and Kurzweil (2005) for an application on transhuman values to human bodies.

the top of the list for favourite movie hero and villain simultaneously (Singer 2008).

Like Lyotard's (1984, xxiv) definition of the postmodern, posthumanism is inclined toward incredulity when it crosses metanarratives. Therefore, the posthuman can be aligned with other approaches and techniques that question universality, rationality, and scientific objectivity. As its very name implicates the post*human* in humanist traditions, using language—as spoken and written language is seen as what makes humans exceptional in the great chain of being—often obfuscates other understandings of the world through affect, art, and desire. Those imagining the posthuman would have to ask if the master's tools could dismantle the master's house (Lorde 2007, 110-114)? This includes discourse, history, science, and technology—at least those birthed from Western civilization are deeply implicated in what the posthuman may desire to leave behind. 'So what of the humanities,' Colebrook (2014, 169-70) queries, 'if anything at all, might we say is worth saving?' Humanism is actually quite inhuman, she answers, but what can posthumanism offer? Perhaps it is contaminated and possessed by the repressed, by all that colonialisms and capitalisms have buried and tried to hide, murder, and torture. The posthuman knows that the subject, as we have created it, has a special relationship to the degradation and dismissal of objects and the objectification of subjects. These distinctions between the two are a story about our modern world-making and this tale of intertwining needs to be retold to create more just and peaceful relationships.

As scholars, we often speak of the posthuman as a noun. Our debates revolve around whether the concept can be housed in some kind of bounded subjectivity that we can define and attach to particular bodies. Can we know it, secure it, nurture it, theorise it, dismiss it, ignore it? Is it cyborg (Haraway 1991, 191)? Zombie (Lauro and Embry 2008)? Fossil (Yusoff 2013)? Android (Dick 1996)? Hybrid (MacCormack 2016; Chen 2012; Lowenhaupt Tsing 2015)? Digital (Adams and Thompson 2016; Gibson 1984)?

Cary Wolfe asked, 'What is posthumanism?' (2010), but for this essay the question becomes: 'What is posthumanising?'

Learning and being open to how to cultivate the conditions to become otherwise: this is posthumanising. We must build the conditions that make the human obsolete; to follow Buckminster Fuller (1970) in *I Seem to Be a Verb*, we can't fight existing reality. We need to create models that make the old ones obsolete. This is systems biology and quantum physics, monism not Cartesian dualism. Most importantly it is interrogating the violence of the nature/culture dichotomy (Morton 2010) and that the distinction between object and subject are not what we thought they were (Gane 2006) or that they were never there (Latour 1993). Following Haraway and Latour, if we have never been human or modern what does it mean to be posthuman?

To answer this, I want to focus on this desire to be something different. Not as teleology, but rather what the process of evolving, either biologically, intellectually, or culturally may mean for our quotidian lives.

To further the feeling of action, the remaining will continue in classic three-act structure. This essay is equal parts tragedy and comedy, as catharsis must come from both grief, for the terrible changes wrought by a fossil fuel economy, and hope that this test will leave us will new skills. This catharsis will give us a sense of who the human might become to better live within our planetary limits: to find 'wild laughter in the throat of death' and use mirth to move our souls to action (Shakespeare 1598).

This figure of the posthuman will disperse into becoming not being, process not product, desire not completion. If not a subject coming into itself, then is it a plea? A plea to a future to hear, to witness that we crave to become *transformed*.

The posthuman is an acknowledgement of the despair and exhaustion wrapped up in what it must mean to be modern, to be human. We are so tired of being what we are now: murderous, hateful, warlike, wasteful, narcissistic, violent, careless, vicious, cruel, and belligerent. Through this shell of the human it becomes hard to move toward the antonymic of that which we are tired of being and enacting.

Posthumanising is not a plea, but a roar to a world that has silenced so many for so long. 'My barbaric yawp,' crowed Walt Whitman (1949, 1088) in 'Song of Myself': 'I too am not a bit tamed—I too am untranslatable; I sound my barbaric yawp over the roof of the world.' Dr. Suess's Horton (1954) the Elephant heard it, too. His ear heard a Yopp! from the Whos as he listened to the clover held in his trunk. That speck of dust on a clover that made noises in greater amounts: 'We are here. We are here. WE ARE HERE...And that Yopp, that one small extra Yopp, put it over, finally at last from that speck on that clover.'

What if this shout and this demand to be heard cannot be a *something* at all? Even more precisely, what if housing this desire, this striving, this yawp in a body has taken us down the wrong path? Put differently, what if the focus is shifted from what the posthuman is to what the posthuman can do? The posthuman is an action word, not a person, place, or thing. Posthumanising is a performance of our desire to change ourselves.

Performing the Posthuman: An Apocapolitical Tragicomedy in Three Acts

Act I: The exposition, or posthumanising ethics

The fundamental ethical question surrounding the posthuman, or how ethics could be posthumanised, is to acknowledge that humans have speciously separated themselves from other living things and processes on the planet and called it *nature*. We then, through religion and dominion, humanism and natural law, turned the earth and its many other beings into resources to be used with no moral, intrinsic worth except that which humans could take and use for their own ends. Other world-views that were counter to this were colonised and even eradicated, leaving this dichotomy with little to stand against it. With this backdrop, the ethical issue most at stake is how we treat other living beings (Waldau 2007).

One of the most serious elisions in much of the posthuman literature is not acknowledging that many humans have been treated as things, objects, and likened to the nonhuman animals we use and abuse. This is unacceptable for both. For those who have not been considered fully human, the posthuman is an intolerable erasing of suffering and violence added to a toxic misunderstanding of world history and the complex relations of power that exist globally from North to South, East to West, black to white, female to male, rich to poor, human to nonhuman animal. These past and present hierarchies will reproduce the same power structures if we are not vigilant.

The posthuman can be recognised as an always already racialised and gendered body born from the flesh of the slave, the incarcerated, the oppressed (Weheliye 2014). It stands opposed the Enlightenment Man and its monopoly on subjectivity based on white, male European bodies (Hayles 1999). The posthuman can shed 'Man's' allegedly neutral and apolitical skin for a rainbow cloak of plurality and multiplicity.

Posthumanising recognises this and moves to create radical solidarity along all lines of difference (Morton 2017). This includes overcoming the human/ nonhuman distinction and nurturing an ethics of entanglement in multispecies communities and co-evolved nonhuman animal companions (Haraway 2003; 2007). Disconnecting ourselves from nature has led toward violence to nonhuman others and legitimates that violence and suffering (Wright 2014). Extending care to nonhumans and thinking across species lines will increase our ability to create deeper cultural and social connections among humans, too (Waldau 2007). Posthumanising will recognise that fighting for the dignity of human and nonhuman animal life will improve the lives of all. Our fates are inextricably linked and all must be protected, honoured, and liberated together. Even if posthumans will think in verbs, we cannot denigrate the noun and we must recognise and celebrate life and things (Bennett 2010).

Posthumanising will be hard work that builds a planetary geontological (Povinelli 2016) politics that does not rest on hidden exclusions and violence. Posthumanising will create healthy diverse communities - human and nonhuman - rather than maximising profit and personal wealth. It becomes paramount to recreate ourselves around a new materialism that values the earth for more than what we can consume from it.

Act II: The conflict, or a compromised biome and ecosystems facing collapse

There is urgency involved in rethinking ourselves: this is not just an exercise in high theory or pedagogy for the classroom. The human and its position on Earth is a topic of much concern in global neoliberal capitalism and those arrayed against its rapacious and utilitarian use of fossil fuels and human capital. It is vitally important that we change who we are. As subjects created for consumption, Earth and its inhabitants are facing an unprecedented crisis. Due to the actions of human beings, the earth has entered a geologic epoch named the Anthropocene. The term was coined by Paul Crutzen in 2002 and has now been recommended for adoption after a prolonged study of human activity on our planetary systems. In September 2016, the International Geological Congress reported that, indeed, due to radioactive materials left by nuclear testing, plastic and power plant pollution, to name but a few, the Anthropocene can now be recognised as a reality. The end of the Holocene—the previous era—is marked by sea level rise, increased carbon dioxide emissions, deforestation, development, and global mass extinction of nonhuman species. The naming of this new era after *anthropos* can be taken as evidence toward our entangled relationship with the planet that provides the conditions for life. It is a view that reminds us of our bodies and connections, rather than the ultimate homage to our self-absorption. As Wright (2014 online) stresses, 'looking at the world from the perspective of the Anthropocene reveals patterns of connection that bind flesh to earth, sea and sky on a multispecies planet.'

Unfortunately, near universal scientific acceptance of this epoch has not been matched politically. The Paris Convention (COP21) agreement in 2015 represents a major international decision on climate change action, but the nature of international treaties leaves it open to failure at the state level: ratification of the treaty must happen in each state and then laws and policies must change to reflect the international commitment. Previously, I, and my co-authors (Burke et al. 2016, 500), have argued that we need a politics to match our planet:

> Global ecological collapse brings new urgency to the claim that 'we are all in this together' – humans, animals, ecologies, biosphere. To survive, we must ask questions that are intimately connected to capitalism, modernity, and oppression. We must ensure that our diplomacy, our politics, and our institutions are open to those who will bear the brunt of ecological change.

Most importantly, this change from noun to verb aids in seeing ourselves as not individuals in the humanist, liberal tradition, but as an active part of an entangled and complex web—or nested sets of permeable vessels—of both human and nonhuman life on a shared planet (Fishel 2017).

Posthumanising will include acknowledging the planetary real and recreating systemic human agency that recognises earth systems and their boundaries. The Anthropocene should be presented as an era that reminds us that we are in it together and not another retelling of the story of dominion over a natural place external to the world of the human.

Act III: The resolution, or posthumanising activism

This focus on posthumanising will emphasise two broad areas as possible avenues for action: the ethical, and the political/disciplinary, through activism. Active posthumanising will mean engaged and direct action in multiple contexts and across multiple registers. Politically, how might posthumanising be deployed into concerns that also support those from ecological, feminist, queer, postcolonialist, and anticapitalist standpoint (Behar 2016)?

Posthumanising academic disciplines remains a challenge. Our very ways of thinking are firmly rooted in humanism and siloed into different disciplines in the modern neoliberal university. This hierarchical and isolated institutional matrix for intellectual work makes asking complex questions across disciplines difficult. There is a clear disciplinary division of labour between the social sciences and the natural sciences. For Andrew Pickering (2005), they carve up the world in systematic ways: the natural sciences study the world of things where people are absent and there is a clear idea of objectivity and a need to understand the systems themselves divorced from the researcher's place in the systems. In the social sciences and humanities, researchers talk about people and not about things with an idea that the social is separate reality from the world of things that natural scientists study. As discussed above, this is a beautiful dualism: world of things and world of people. The posthuman view, according to Pickering (2005), is that which allows us to 'see double', to overlap people and things in our research programs, matters of concern, and telling of events. Posthumanising the disciplines will have us reject these units of analysis because the world does not impose that division of people and things on us. We make the world and impose legibility upon it. The units of analysis can be shifted, the posthuman can see double (Pickering 2005).

The tragedy and scale of destruction brought on by climate change challenges all of our political systems and institutions. Do we need to learn how to die as a species, as Roy Scranton (2015) declares? Or, as Naomi Klein (2014) argues, do we need to take up the challenge of the climate crisis as our best chance at creating a new world, and see that crisis as causing a fracture in our collective subjectivity that will allow us to tear through to new relations and practices? The nation-state will continue to decline under ecological crisis and cannot offer solutions that it had claimed to in the last century. In this assertion, Klein (2014) echoes Guattari's writing on the ecological crisis. He wrote: 'Instead of clinging to general recommendations we would be implementing effective practices of experimentation, as much on a microsocial level as on a larger institutional scale' (Guattari 2008, 24). Change will happen from the grassroots level. While global level change is necessary, it must be fought and redefined at the level of specific practices and sites, like Standing Rock. In other words, planetary change could lead to the discovering of the creative potential of people – in all parts of the world and from all social positions – to reshape the priorities of regions, states, and economies (Connolly 2017).

We can think of Fuller's (1970, 1) famous quote: 'I live on Earth at present, and I don't know what I am. I know that I am not a category. I am not a thing — a noun. I seem to be a verb, an evolutionary process — an integral function of the universe.'

If used as a starting point, the posthuman could see this rephrased for the Anthropocene: 'I live in love with the Earth and its beings, and I am always becoming what I am. I know that I am a category. I am enmeshed—a thing living entwined with other things. I seem to be a verb, an ever changing process—a cosmic roll of the universal dice.'

This crisis could be the beginning. It is our last, and best chance, to make another world rather than just mutely witness the end of our fossil-fuelled civilization. If last century was more about freeing the carbon than it was about freeing humanity from its chains (Wark 2015), this century could be able to understand our posthuman condition, and build new kin groups (Haraway 2016) in such a way that a world could emerge that is more equitable, loving, and just than the last.

References

Adams, Catherine, and Terrie Lynn Thompson. 2016. *Researching a Posthuman World: Interviews with Digital Objects* London: Palgrave.

Behar, Katherine. 2016. *Object Oriented Feminism.* Minneapolis: University of Minnesota Press.

Bennett, Jane. 2010. *Vibrant Matter: A Political Ecology of Things.* Raleigh: Duke University Press.

Braidotti, Rosi. 2013. *The Posthuman* Cambridge: Polity Press.

Braidotti, Rosi. 2006. "Posthuman, All Too Human: Toward a New Process Ontology." *Theory, Culture, and Society* 23 (7-8): 197-208.

Burke, Anthony, Stefanie Fishel, Audra Mitchell, Simon Dalby, and Daniel J. Levine. 2016. "Planet Politics: A Manifesto from the End of IR." *Millennium: A Journal of International Studies* 44 (3): 499 – 523.

Carretero-Gonzalez, Margarita. 2016. "The Posthuman That Could Have Been: Mary Shelley's Creature." *Relations* 4 (1): 53-64.

Chen, Mel Y., 2012. *Animacies: Biopolitics, Racial Mattering, and Queer Affect.* Raleigh: Duke University Press.

Colebrook, Claire. 2014. *The Death of the Posthuman: Essays on Extinction.* Ann Arbor: Open Humanities Press.

Connolly, William E., 2017. *Facing the Planetary: Entangled Humanism and the Politics of Swarming.* Raleigh: Duke University Press.

Dick, Philip K., 1996. *Do Androids Dream of Electric Sheep?* New York: Ballantine Books.

Fishel, Stefanie. 2017. *The Microbial State: Global Thriving and the Body Politic.* Minneapolis: University of Minnesota Press.

Fuller, Buckminster. 1970. *I Seem to Be a Verb.* New York: Bantam Books.

Gane, Nicholas. 2006. "When We Have Never Been Human, What is to be Done? An Interview with Donna Haraway." *Theory, Culture, and Society* 23 (7-8): 135-158.

Theodor Suess Geisel. 1954. *Horton Hears a Who!* New York: Random House.

Gibson, William. 1984. *Neuromancer.* New York: Ace Books.

Guattari, Felix. 2008. *The Three Ecologies.* London: Continuum.

Haraway, Donna. 2016. *Staying with the Trouble: Making Kin in the Chthulucene.* Raleigh: Duke University Press.

Haraway, Donna. 2007. *When Species Meet.* Minneapolis: University of Minnesota Press.

Haraway, Donna. 2003 *Companion Species Manifesto: Dogs, People, and Significant Otherness.* Chicago: Prickly Paradigm Press.

Haraway, Donna. 1991. *Simians, Cyborgs, and Women: The Reinvention of Nature.* New York: Routledge.

Hayles, Katherine N., 1999. *How We Became Posthuman.* Chicago: the University of Chicago Press.

Klein, Naomi. 2014. *This Changes Everything.* New York: Simon and Schuster.

Kurzweil, Ray. 2005. *The Singularity is Near.* New York: Viking Press.

Latour, Bruno. 1993. *We Have Never Been Modern.* Cambridge: Harvard University Press.

Lauro, Sarah Juliet, and Karen Embry. 2008. "A Zombie Manifesto: The Nonhuman Condition in the Era of Advanced Capitalism." *boundary 2* 35 (1): 85-108.

Lorde, Audre. 2007. "The Master's Tools Will Never Dismantle the Master's House." In *Sister Outsider: Essays and Speeches.* Berkeley: Crossing Press.

Lowenhaupt Tsing, Anna. 2015. *The Mushroom at the End of the World: On the Possibility of Life in the Capitalist Ruins.* Princeton: Princeton University Press.

Lyotard, Jean-François. 1984. *The Postmodern Condition.* Minneapolis: University of Minnesota Press.

MacCormack, Patricia. 2016. *Posthuman Ethics: Embodiment and Cultural Theory.* London and New York: Routledge

Massumi, Brian. 2014. *What Animals Can Teach Us About Politics.* Raleigh: Duke University Press.

Mitchell, Audra. 2014. "Only Human: A Worldly Approach to Security." *Security Dialogue* 45 (1): 5-21.

Morton, Timothy. 2017. *Humankind: Solidarity with Nonhuman People.* London: Verso Books.

Morton, Timothy. 2010. *The Ecological Thought.* Harvard: Harvard University Press.

Parikka, Jussi. 2015. "Cultural forces: Contemporary land arts, technology and new materialist aesthetics." *Cultural Studies Review* 21 (2): 47-75.

Pickering, Andrew. 2005. "Asian Eels and Global Warming: A Posthumanist Perspective on Society and the Environment." *Ethics and the Environment* 10 (2): 29-43.

Povinelli, Elizabeth A., 2016. *Geontologies: A Requiem to Late Liberalism.* Raleigh: Dune University Press.

Scranton, Roy. 2015. *Learning to Die in the Anthropocene: Reflections on the End of a Civilization.* San Francisco: City Lights Books.

Shakespeare, William. 1598. *Love's Labour's Lost.*

Shapin, Steven and Simon Schaffer. 1985. *Leviathan and the Air-Pump: Hobbes, Boyle, and the Experimental Life.* Princeton: Princeton University Press.

Singer, Peter W., 2008. "Robots at War." *Wilson Quarterly* 30 (2): 30-48.

Waldau, Paul. 2007. "Kweli ndugu yanga—the Religious Horizons of "Humans Are Primates." *Worldviews* 11 (1): 103-123.

Wark, McKenzie. 2015. *Molecular Red: Theory for the Anthropocene.* London and New York: Verso Books.

Weheliye, Alexander G., 2014. *Habeas Viscus: Racialising Assemblages, Biopolitics, and Black Feminist Theories of the Subject.* Raleigh: Duke University Press.

Whitman, Walt. 1949. *The Poetry and Prose of Walt Whitman.* New York: Simon and Schuster.

Wolfe, Cary. 2010. *What is Posthumanism.* Minneapolis: University of Minnesota Press.

Wright, Kate. 2014. "An Ethics of Entanglement for the Anthropocene." *Scan: Journal of Media Arts Culture* 11 (1)

Yusoff, Kathryn. 2013. "Geologic life: prehistory, climate, futures in the Anthropocene." *Environment and Planning D: Society and Space* 31 (5): 779 – 795.

Part Two

ECOLOGY, NONHUMAN SPECIES AND THE ANTHROPOCENE

6

Ecological Security

MATT MCDONALD

In recent years, the idea that issues such as climate change might pose a threat to security has become prominent, and environmental issues more broadly have featured significantly in debates about redefining security since the 1980s (Mathews 1989; Myers 1989).

Traditionally, approaches to the relationship between security and environmental change have asked whether and how environmental issues constitute a security threat. This is a bad place to start, for two reasons. First, it suggests that we as analysts can establish criteria for defining security at an abstract level, and measure issues (whether climate change, population displacement or terrorism) against that criteria. Such an approach is problematic. It ignores the social construction of security: the fact that different political communities understand security in different ways, and the same political communities change the way they understand security over time. A fixed and abstract definition of security is ultimately inconsistent with the need to come to terms with the meaning given to security in practice (see McDonald 2012). This is important because of the politics of security: the ways in which different depictions of security and threat serve to encourage particular sets of responses to those issues in practice.

Second, and of particular relevance for those interested in the politics of linking environmental issues with security, the effects of this linkage are not simply about whether environmental issues are defined as a security threat: whether they are 'securitised'. Paradoxically, the view that the designation of threat defines the politics of a response to it is evident among both advocates and sceptics of an environment-security relationship. For advocates, defining environmental issues as security threats means approaching these issues as 'high politics', ensuring political urgency, prioritization and funding usually associated with traditional security threats (see Hartmann 2008). Securitization, in this view, is ultimately a good thing. For sceptics, securitization is problematic because security has a powerful and sedimented association with defence and the state (eg Deudney 1990), and/or potentially enables the suspension of 'normal politics' and the pursuit of frequently illiberal emergency measures. The latter is, of course, a key concern of so-called Copenhagen School theorists of securitization (eg Buzan et al 1998; Wæver 1995).

Yet ultimately, the political implications of linking environmental issues like climate change with security are determined not by the simple act of making this link- of securitising. Rather, what matters in political and normative terms is the *way* security itself is understood. Specifically, different discourses of security- conceptions of whose security matters, from what threats, which agents are responsible for providing it and through what means- have radically different implications in terms of the practices they encourage. While a discourse orienting towards national security might encourage adaptation and even military preparedness for potential conflict associated with the effects of environmental change, a discourse orienting towards human security would encourage mitigation strategies and a focus on the threats facing vulnerable human populations (see McDonald 2012; 2013). In these senses, linking climate change and security can have radically different effects depending on the way in which security is understood, and especially different answers to the question of *whose* security matters.

Using the example of climate change, this paper is divided into two sections. In the first I outline the contours of different discourses of security as applied to climate change, illustrating the ethical choices upon which these discourses are based and pointing to the practices they encourage. In the second I make a case for an ecological security discourse. Simply, if a linkage between an issue like climate change and security is to be made, some discourses are better than others in terms of the defensibility of the principles they are informed by and the responses they suggest. Here I suggest that the most defensible ethical foundation for this linkage is one that focuses on ecosystem resilience and the rights and needs of vulnerable contemporary populations, future generations and other living beings. While such a discourse confronts important dilemmas and powerful political impediments, it is one that rests on a stronger moral and philosophical foundation. And perhaps more importantly, it is a discourse arguably necessitated by the scale of the threat posed by climate change and the changing nature of our relationship to the environment in the context of the Anthropocene: the contemporary geological era in which humans have altered the earth system upon which humans themselves depend (see Steffan et al 2007, as well as Corry, Harrington and Rothe in this volume).

Discourses of Climate Security

There is a range of different ways in which environmental change generally, and climate change specifically, could be and have been linked to security. The most powerful and prominent of these discourses is that of 'national security', with the focus here on the possibility that climate change might undermine the sovereignty or territorial integrity of the nation-state. Such a vision has found its way into national security strategies throughout the world, has been advanced by public-policy oriented think tanks (especially in the USA), and has achieved a prominent place in academic debates (see Brzoska 2008; Busby 2008; CNA 2007).

In such a vision of security, the state retains its central role as the referent object (the 'whom' in 'security for whom'); the state and potentially its military are key agents of security; threats are associated largely with conflict or border integrity arising from climate change; and means of providing security focus on adaptation to manifestations of threat (Busby 2008). Perhaps the starkest example of this discourse, and its limitations, was a 2003 Pentagon Report prepared by Schwartz and Randall (2003) examining the potential national security implications of an abrupt climate change scenario for the United States. In the report, the authors made the claim that some relatively self-sufficient states like the US might seek to build more effective boundaries around the state to prevent those displaced by climate change – environmental refugees – from entering.

This example clearly constitutes a perverse response to climate change. Victims of climate change are presented as potential threats; the focus is exclusively on adaptation, not mitigation; there is no focus on the rights of vulnerable populations; and no genuine possibility – consistent with the Realist tradition in which this discourse is located – for international cooperation to address this global problem (see Dalby 2009). Certainly, this approach would endorse the concerns of those sceptics opposed to the securitization of climate change.

More recently, a range of efforts have been made to link climate change to international security. Here, the emphasis is on the possibility that climate change might undermine international stability or challenge the normative basis of an international society. The nature of the climate threat is its possible contribution to large-scale humanitarian crises, population displacement and even international conflict. This was the subject of debates in the UN Security Council in 2007 and 2011, and this discourse has also been taken up by think tanks and NGOs (see Smith and Vivekananda 2007). Most recently it has been prominent in linkages made between climate change and conflict in Syria and even the emergence of Daesh (see Baker 2015; Strozier and Berkell 2015), building on earlier linkages between climate change and conflict in Darfur (see UNEP 2007; Ki Moon 2007). The referent object of security is international society; threats are threats to international order and stability associated with climate change; agents are largely defined in terms of key international institutions; and means of security are ultimately cooperative international efforts focused on a combination of mitigation and adaptation (see Purvis and Busby 2004).

The emphasis here on the possibility of international cooperation, the suggestion of some role for prevention (i.e. mitigation) and the general sense that a moral universe extends beyond the nation-state suggests progress from a national security discourse. Yet this discourse remains closely linked to the preservation of the state system, a position with potentially problematic ethical foundations and implications. Of course at a practical level, an international state system has - at best - responded inadequately to the problem of climate change to date, with current mitigation commitments inadequate for preventing dangerous climate change and global climate cooperation erring consistently towards the lowest common denominator in international negotiations (see Stevenson and Dryzek 2014; Eckersley 2017). At worst, the international system has helped drive processes of global climate change through endorsing and enabling the neoliberal economic order, which has driven rapid industrialization and over-consumption. While a step forward in linking climate change and security, then, we might ask whether the international system is fit for purpose in addressing climate change, and whether the vision of international society in this international security discourse is ultimately one worth preserving (see McDonald 2013).

A more radical climate security discourse focuses on climate change as a threat to human security. For advocates of this discourse, climate change already poses a threat to human security, defined in terms of peoples' survival and their capacity to pursue meaningful, sustainable lives in the face of climate change (see Barnett et al 2010). This approach has been more marginal to international practice than the above discourses, but has been advanced by NGO groups, was explicitly endorsed by the UNDP (2007) and in a 2009 UN General Assembly discussion of the climate change-security relationship, and was the subject of a chapter in the most recent IPCC report on the impacts of climate change (IPCC 2014). The referent object in this discourse is people; threats are those that challenge the lives, livelihoods and choices of people; means of security focus on mitigation but with some place for adaptation; and a wide variety of actors – from states to international institutions to civil society groups – are seen as potential security agents (see O'Brien 2006).

In orienting towards the direct and immediate effects of climate change for people, and focusing our attention on vulnerable human populations, the human security discourse advances a more ethically defensible position in the context of climate change. The practices it encourages are also focused on preventing the worst manifestations of climate change through urgent mitigation action, and reducing the threat for those most vulnerable. Yet there are clear dilemmas or challenges here. First, it is difficult to assess and redress sources of human insecurity in the context of climate change given both varied populations with possibly competing interests, and acute uncertainty and complexity with regard to climate change and its effects. Second, and in the context of agency, a focus on vulnerable human populations requires international institutions and the most powerful states to act as agents for others and beyond their own immediate self-interest. Both of these challenges apply to the ecological security discourse, to be discussed.

Clearly, this discourse constitutes a progressive approach to the climate-security relationship, one whose orientation towards vulnerable people is far more defensible than approaches that value the defence of institutions or already privileged populations, and whose practices orient primarily towards mitigation rather than adaptation alone. Yet it still draws the line at contemporary human populations, in this context failing to recognise obligations to future generations or other living beings. And in endorsing a humanist approach, arguably this discourse fails to recognise and respond to the changing nature of our relationship to the environment in the context of the Anthropocene (Grove 2014). A case can therefore be made for a more radical climate security discourse still - one oriented towards ecological security.

Towards Ecological Security

Ultimately, existing discourses of 'climate security' orient towards the preservation of contemporary forms of human communities, whether defined in national, international or genuinely *human* terms. Some of these discourses are clearly more progressive than others in encouraging action oriented towards genuinely addressing the problem itself; recognising obligations to vulnerable communities; and even suggesting the need for urgent and rapid change to redress the challenges posed by climate change. Yet the climate crisis arguably suggests the need for yet more radical reorientation of ethical principles and urgent sets of practices than that articulated in the above discourses. And the narrative of the Anthropocene serves too to point to the need to fundamentally re-examine the distinctions between humanity and nature that arguably underpin all the discourses of security noted above. But if a shift towards a genuinely ecological security discourse appears needed, what are the key contours of this approach to climate security?

An ecological security discourse is one that orients towards the resilience of ecosystems themselves, in turn enabling the protection of the most vulnerable across time, space and species. Resilience is defined in terms of the capacity of ecosystems to sustain life, and retain their organizational structure and function in the face of perturbation and change (see Barnett 2001; Adger et al 2011). Urgent mitigation action is prioritised in this discourse but with some space for adaptation to help preserve the functionality of ecosystems. All actors with the capacity to generate avoidable harm have responsibility in terms of agency, depending on their capacity and contribution to the problem. And while endorsing broad principles, such a discourse must be defined in terms of a commitment to dialogue, reflexivity and humility: ecosystem functionality is too complex for highly prescriptive accounts; universal principles must be reconciled with local knowledge, understanding and values; and reflexivity is clearly necessary to prevent this discourse from becoming a repressive or misanthropic orthodoxy. What we are talking about here, ultimately, is a set of principles that might be defended as an appropriate basis for actors to view and approach the climate change-security relationship, with the actions this encourages necessarily context-specific.

Such a discourse has not been prominent in either academic debate or political interventions linking climate change and security. Of course, this may reflect the fact that it has a limited constituency among those with power (see Barnett 2001:121), and that we can clearly advocate progressive approaches to climate change without recourse to the language of security. Yet as the climate security link is increasingly made in academic and policy circles, with climate change featuring in UNSC debates and in national security strategies of states throughout the world (Scott 2015), it is important to examine the form and likely implications of this linkage. In this context, we need to consider the contours of a more progressive approach in terms of both the principles upon which it is based and the practices it encourages. Simply, if the 'securitization' of climate change is becoming more common, we cannot ignore the climate-security relationship. Instead, and reflecting the political significance of security (see Browning and McDonald 2013; Wæver 1995), we need to ask how these linkages are made, whose security is considered important, what a progressive linkage (with defensible principles and progressive implications in practice) might look like and what prospects exist for such a discourse to be articulated, embraced and even institutionalised.

A shift towards the embrace of an ecological security discourse in the context of climate change might be difficult to imagine, but it might be one necessitated by a number of factors. First, it is difficult to justify an exclusive ethical focus on contemporary human populations, especially those limited to particular spatial areas. Drawing on holistic ethics and some insights of ecological perspectives (eg Naess 1989) and critical political ecology (see Eckersley 2005), an ecological security discourse challenges the idea of limiting our ethical boundaries to currently living human populations and encourages us to consider the rights and needs of others – now and into the future – who rely on the continued function of those ecosystems. Second, and related to this, the new reality of the Anthropocene encourages us to revisit the relationship between humanity and the conditions of our own survival. The Anthropocene arguably requires us to revisit the separation between humans and nature central to contemporary political thought and action, and recognise that we can no longer orient our security towards the conservation of the status quo (see also Mitchell 2014; Grove 2014).

There are, of course, profound challenges and dilemmas associated with this discourse. If our focus is ecosystem resilience in the face of change, means of security would emphasise mitigation but potentially extend to controversial practices focused on adaptation and stop-gap measures, including geoengineering. Dilemmas here are immediately apparent. First, such projects are frequently advocated by those who want to support a continued role for fossil fuels. Second, pursuing geoengineering strategies can involve the search for a climate change 'silver bullet', rather than profound changes necessary in the way we live (see Dalby 2015). And third, the scale of complexity and uncertainty that is a defining feature of ecosystem functionality makes it exceedingly difficult to be certain about what the implications of our interventions will be and therefore what practices we should pursue (see Cudworth and Hobden 2013). This becomes even more complicated when trying to weigh potentially competing interests across populations, species and over time.

Even if we are confident about what sets of practices an ecological security discourse would encourage, it clearly has a limited political constituency and limited political traction. If it is difficult enough to get states to cooperate with other states to solve a problem that affects them, some might suggest it is impossible to imagine how an approach oriented towards other living beings or future generations will find its way into meaningful public debate (Barnett 2001). And finally, the tendency to articulate universal principles must confront the challenges of negotiating with local practices and localised understandings of ecosystems themselves.

All of the above do represent profound challenges in making sense of what an ecological security discourse might look like and even whether it is defensible. But the extent to which these dilemmas are particular to this discourse should not be overstated. Even national security discourses have to come to terms with uncertainty and complexity in terms of assessing where future strategic threats might come from and how state resources should be used to prepare for these, for example. The dangers of reconciling universal principles with local contexts are all too familiar to advocates of international security, whose attempts to manage peace operations must always negotiate this divide (Paris and Sisk eds. 2009). And in trying to combine a case for change with the need to enlist powerful actors to be agents of that change, human security discourses always risk being coopted by those institutions without fundamentally reorienting their practices or the basis upon which they make decisions (see Christie 2010). And perhaps obviously, political limits to change confront all those advocating change, almost all the time.

Yet we have clearly seen major changes in dominant understandings and practices of security over time, from the redefinition of sovereignty as the responsibility to protect to the endorsement of nuclear disarmament. These should serve as reminders that change can and does happen, and advocates of ecological security might find bases for hope in the embrace of principles like precaution, common but differentiated responsibility, debates arising around the Anthropocene and the global, long-term and ecological orientation of much of global civil society mobilization. And by linking climate change and security, the profound nature of the challenge posed by climate change arguably compels us to think in new ways about what security means and how it might be realised.

References

Adger, W. Neil, Katrina Brown and James Waters. 2011. "Resilience" in John Dryzek, Richard Norgaard and David Schlosberg, eds., *The Oxford Handbook of Climate Change and Society*. Oxford: Oxford UP.

Baker, Aryn. 2015. "How climate change is behind the surge of migrants to Europe", *Time Magazine*, http://time.com/4024210/climate-change-migrants/. September 7.

Barnett, Jon et al. 2010. "Global Environmental change and human security" in Richard Matthew et al, eds., *Global Environmental Change and Human Security.* Cambridge, Mass: MIT Press.

Barnett, Jon. 2001. *The Meaning of Environmental Security*. London: Zed Books.

Browning, Christopher S., and Matt Mcdonald. 2013. "The Future of Critical Security Studies: Ethics and the Politics of Security" *European Journal of International Relations* 19(2): 235-255.

Brzoska, Michael. 2008. "The Securitization of Climate Change and the Power of Conceptions of Security", Paper Presented at *International Studies Association Convention*, San Francisco, March 2008.

Busby, Joshua. 2008. "Who Cares about the Weather? Climate Change and US National Security" *Security Studies* 17(3): 468-504.

Buzan, Barry; Ole Wæver and Jaap de Wilde. 1998. *Security: A New Framework for Analysis*. Boulder, Colorado: Lynne Rienner.

Christie, Ryerson. 2010. "Critical Voices and Human Security: To Endure, To Engage or To Critique?" *Security Dialogue* 41(2): 169-190.

CNA. 2007. *National Security and the Threat of Climate Change*. Washington DC: CNA.

Cudworth, Erika and Stephen Hobden. 2013. 'Complexity, Ecologism and Posthuman Politics" *Review of International Studies* 39 (3): 643-664.

Dalby, Simon. 2015. "Geoengineering: The Next Era of Geopolitics?" *Geography Compass* 9(4): 190-201.

Dalby, Simon. 2009. *Security and Environmental Change.* Cambridge: Polity.

Dalby, Simon. 2007. "Anthropocene Geopolitics: Globalisation, Empire, Environment and Critique" *Geography Compass* 1(1): 103–118.

Deudney, Daniel. 1990. "The case against linking environmental degradation and national security" *Millennium: Journal of International Studies* 19(3): 461-73.

Eckersley, Robyn (2017) 'Who's Afraid of a Climate Treaty?' in Gaita and Simpson, *Who's Afraid of International Law?* (Melbourne: Monash UP).

Eckersley, Robyn. 2005. "Ecocentric Discourses: Problems and Future Prospects for Nature Advocacy" in Dryzek, John and David Schlosberg, eds., *Debating the Earth: A Reader*, 2nd ed. Oxford: Oxford UP.

Gleick, Peter H. 2014. "Water, Drought, Climate Change, and Conflict in Syria", *Weather Climate and Society*, 6: 331–340.

Grove, Jairus V. 2014. "Ecology as critical security method" *Critical Studies on Security* 2(3): 366-369.

Hartmann, Betsy. 2009. "Lines in the Shifting Sand: The Strategic Politics of Climate Change, Human Security and National Defence" Paper presented at *Rethinking Security in a Changing Climate Conference*, Oslo, June 2009.

IPCC. 2014. *Climate Change 2014: Impacts, Adaptation and Vulnerability.* Cambridge: Cambridge UP.

Ki-Moon, Ban. 2007. "A climate culprit in Darfur" *Washington Post*, 16 June.

Mathews, Jessica Tuchman. 1989. "Redefining Security" *Foreign Affairs*, 68(2): 162-77.

McDonald, Matt. 2013. "Discourses of Climate Security" *Political Geography*, 33: 43-51.

McDonald, Matt. 2012. *Security, the Environment and Emancipation: Contestation over Environmental Change.* London: Routledge.

Mitchell, Audra. 2014. "Only Human? A Worldly Approach to Security" *Security Dialogue* 45(1): 5-21.

Myers, Norman. 1989. "Environment and Security" *Foreign Policy* 74: 23-41.

Naess, Arne. 1989. *Ecology, Community and Lifestyle.* Cambridge: Cambridge UP.

O'Brien, Karen. 2006. "Are we Missing the Point? Global Environmental Change as an Issue of Human Security" *Global Environmental Change*, 16(1):1-3.

Oels, Andrea. 2012. "From Securitization of Climate Change to Climatization of the Security Field" in J. Scheffran, eds., *Climate Change, Human Security and Violent Conflict*. Berlin: Springer.

Paris, Roland and Timothy Sisk. eds. 2009. *The Dilemmas of Statebuilding.* London: Routledge.

Purvis, Nigel and Joshua Busby (2004) 'The Security Implications of Climate Change for the UN System', *Environmental Change and Security Project Report*, 10: 67-73.

Scott, Shirley. 2015. "Implications of climate change for the UN Security Council," *International Affairs* 91 (5): 1317-33.

Schwartz, Peter and Doug Randall. 2003. "An Abrupt Climate Change Scenario and its Implications for United States National Security" *Global Business Network*, October, Online at: http://www.gbn.com/consulting/article_ details.php?id=53.

Smith, Dan and Janani Vivekananda. 2007. *A Climate of Conflict: The Links between Climate Change, Peace and War.* London: International Alert.

Steffan, Will, Paul Crutzen and John McNeill. 2007. "The Anthropocene: Are Humans Now Overwhelming the Great Forces of Nature?" *Ambio*, 36(8): 614-21.

Stevenson, Hayley and John S. Dryzek. 2014. *Democratising Global Climate Governance.* Cambridge: Cambridge UP.

Strozier, Charles B and Kelly A. Berkell. 2014. "How climate change helped ISIS" in *Huffington Post,* 29 September http://www.huffingtonpost.com/ charles-b-strozier/how-climate-change-helped_b_5903170.html, accessed 25/04/17.

UNDP. 2007. *Fighting Climate Change : Human Solidarity in a Divided World.* New York: Palgrave.

UNEP. 2007. *Sudan: Post-Conflict Environmental Assessment.* Nairobi: UNEP.

Wæver, Ole. 1995. "Securitization and de-securitization" in Ronnie D. Lipschutz, eds. *On Security.* New York: Columbia UP.

7

Posthuman Security and Care in the Anthropocene

CAMERON HARRINGTON

As many of the authors in this collection make clear, traditional and critical ideas about security have been largely anthropocentric. Whether the focus has been on the strategic manoeuvrings of states acting in relation to balances of power, or on the performative effects of security discourses, all security has been human security. To speak of security absent the human subject has been considered irrational or worse, uninteresting.

Recently though, this perspective has been shifting, thanks in large part to a growing alertness to the diverse forms of life that produce and are affected by conditions of (in)security. In an ironic twist, this nascent posthuman sensibility is deeply connected to the realization that we have entered into a monumental period of global environmental change enacted by humans. The Anthropocene – the Age of (hu)Man – has garnered enormous amounts of attention across the natural sciences, social sciences, and humanities. Beyond encapsulating the environmental catastrophe that is unfolding before us, a central motif of Anthropocene thinking, as it has been translated from geological stratigraphy, is the collapse of the divide between the social and the natural. As the human population explodes and we settle into a new world that may be four degrees warmer by century's end, we are obliged to accept not simply the status of humans as geological agents, but as entangled agents.

This reimagining explodes the western, Cartesian belief in dualism, whereby minds and bodies are separated along with the spiritual and the material, humans and nature: the inside/outside divides that have been so central to security studies (Walker 1993). This dualism is justified principally via a belief in radically separated reason, which allows for humans to appear different, outside and above an inferiorised and manipulable nature (Plumwood 2002). The effects of this dualism are to present humans as rational, acting, agents fulfilling their desires in a passive, intentional, global environment. The poverty of these 'Cartesian coordinates' has been highlighted for decades in security studies. These critiques have been presented primarily in terms of the breakdown of the Westphalian system and the exploration of alternative political identities beyond the state – such as nations, races, classes, movements, religions, cultures, or gender (Walker 1993). The Anthropocene further breaks down the divide not simply in terms of political identity but by emphasising the ways that non-human species, technologies, and natures interact with global security (Harrington 2016). The Human Age compels us to question prevailing forms of anthropocentrism and confront the power of other-than-human things in the world.

Readers may wonder what, if anything, can be done? As the recent 'Planet Politics Manifesto' laments, 'Trying to write from within IR, we find ourselves prisoners in our own vocation. We are speechless, or even worse, cannot find words to represent the world and those within it.' (Burke, Fishel, Mitchell, Dalby, and Levine 2016, 502) If everything changes in the Anthropocene - the objects of study, the variety of harms, the nature of responsibility – what is left? Is security obsolete or powerless in the face of Earth system changes? Should we move to something else - perhaps resilience, or quantum politics, or some form of risk theory? Can posthuman security perspectives really transcend the IR 'prison' or will they simply replicate its Holocene-bred, anthropocentric logics within an expanded circle of concern? This article argues against either the abandonment of security or its reduction to its solely negative or positive forms. Instead, it prompts us to cultivate new (and activate very old) forms of care-based security. The new world of the Anthropocene and the posthuman sensibilities that arise from it offer us simultaneous and conflicting impulses. Given the reality that the Earth at once offers a safe haven for existence and poses formidable challenges for life and the capacities for collective human action, security politics might return to the ultimate horizon – the impulse to care.[20]

Security and Care

The Anthropocene is indeed a crisis, both in material terms and, far less importantly, for the study of security. Grasping the idea of the Earth as both a unified system and as something with multiple states of being with imperceptible, shifting, and seeping thresholds is a terrifyingly difficult process (Clark 2016, 139). It offers us little hope that life within it will be any better for

---

[20]   To whom or what we extend care is open-ended and might include life, non-life, and technology.

most humans and our non-human kin. Yet, to reduce the future to apocalyptic visions of flooded cities, charred farmlands and waves of migrants battling for access to ever-dwindling resources in the developed world is a mythical replay of Hobbesian-inspired security forms that should have long ago been abandoned. The Anthropocene should likewise not be reduced to some innate benevolence of a whole system that is designed either by chance or design to protect humans. Given the violent and dynamic tendencies of the planet, there is a need to challenge the feminised image of Gaia, so prevalent in Anthropocene discourse, which portrays the Earth system as a bountiful goddess or a nurturing mother, able to provide for all life, including humans, so long as we protect and sustain her natural state. As Latour reminds us, the Earth system (Gaia) is both nurturing and destructive. She is not indifferent because she is so clearly affected by human behaviour. But She has aims that directly produce human insecurity and civilizational collapse. She is simultaneously '...too fragile to play the calming role of old nature, too unconcerned by our destiny to be a Mother, too unable to be propitiated by deals and sacrifices to be a Goddess.' (Latour 2011)

If we are to focus on cultivating a different form of security, one that is post-human, post-natural, and that does not rely upon Holocene-bred logics, where might we turn? Can we end up avoiding all that and still call it *security*? While I am aware of the difficulty of answering that question here, I argue that security will likely remain a necessary component of adjusting to the Anthropocene. Despite this, we are forced to reconsider the traditional obsession with tragedy (which is everywhere in Anthropocene discourse) and instead focus on care. The notion of care attunes us to the shifting contours of life and death in the Anthropocene. A security that is caring and careful preserves the concept's historical coherence. It also emphasises the relational practices that underpin the survival and flourishing of life in addition to embracing and accepting the finality of earthly existence in the Anthropocene. Finally, supporting multi-perspective forms of care action helps amend traditional security ethics like autonomy, non-interference and reciprocity.

It may seem counterintuitive, but security has always been concerned with the concept of care. Indeed, if we refer back to Heidegger, it is care that motivates human being-in-the-world (what he refers to as Dasein) in the first place. It is care that makes existence visible (Heidegger 1978). Likewise, the concept of security is at a fundamental level about the human relationship to care. John T. Hamilton expertly explains in his book *Security: Politics, Humanity and the Philology of Care* that our concern for security is ultimately a concern to be without concern (2013, 10). We have struggled to reconcile this from the earliest beginning of the security concept, which was formed via Roman fables of the character *Cura*, the personification of care and concern.

From *Cura* comes the etymological root of security, *securitas*, which translates into modern English as the state of being removed from care; the state of being care-free. Hamilton explains,

> The word is transparent enough, featuring three distinct components: the prefix *sē-* (apart, aside, away from); the noun *cura* (care, concern, attention, worry); and the suffix-*tas* (denoting a condition or state of being). Securitas, therefore, denotes a condition of being separated from care, a state wherein concerns and worries have been put off to the side. Man will be literally secure when he is removed from Cura's governance, when his unified being is split apart, back into its discrete elements (2013, 5).

This reading tells us that the desire for security – understood as certitude and trust – is seemingly universal and timeless. We all seek to reduce uncertainty and the risk of personal harm it brings. *Securitas* is an ideal state where there is no risk and care is no longer needed; where we can exist in serene tranquility, without worry and with the knowledge that no harm is coming. Yet, the flip side of the security-care relationship points to an inherent contradiction.

> ...*Securitas* can just as well refer to 'indifference' (the lack of interest) or 'negligence' (the lack of concern for a person or object). By removing *cura* as commitment or concentrated effort, by ignoring the loved one or neglecting one's work, the elimination of care denotes 'heedlessness,' implying that one is no longer driven by the concerns that are believed to define and guide human existence, moral behavior, or practical action. Free from these kinds of concern, we are secure in the sense of being inattentive or indifferent, foolhardy or delinquent. In this case, the privation of devoted attention threatens to leave us deprived (Hamilton 2013, 11).

From its earliest beginnings care has played a central role in security and the desire to eradicate care continues to drive our security decisions. Yet Hamilton also makes clear that the contours of security have always been contested. He weaves in a variety of sources, from ancient Greek poetry to Roman stoicism, from Hobbes to Schmitt and Heidegger, to underline the 'vast network of mythical, linguistic, and cultural valences and traditions that have motivated the term's usage across histories' (Hamilton 2013, 276). Given the unique ability of the Anthropocene to dissolve the promise of security, more care, not less, is needed in the posthuman, postnatural

Anthropocene.

The Origins of Care

Part of the modern invocation to care derives from the well-established feminist paradigm of care ethics. At its core, care ethics is about concrete, particular, relationships. Humans should pursue moral action based upon their empathic consideration of the other they exist in relation to. This perspective deemphasises the traditional view that ethics should be derived from the rational invocation of universal duties, responsibilities, or principles. It also rejects attempts to impose Newtonian laws upon social relations. In place of this it asks us to consider the unique value of relationships and ongoing, shifting patterns of interactions and responses. This means being cognizant of the needs, wants, and desires of the 'world,' defined as one's self, loved ones, near and distant others, society, and the planet (Engster 2004, 117). Occupying a moral position requires that we adopt 'actions and attitudes of care, in addition to or even more importantly than those of respect, non-interference, and tit-for-tat reciprocity...' (Collins 2015, 5). Care then becomes an approach to life that recognises the needs of others, attempts to respond to/provide for those needs, and establishes relationships of trust that transcend the boundaries of justice. This centres the social and the unequal power relationships that define life in the Anthropocene - moving beyond critique to advocate 'new forms of relationships, institutions, and actions that enhance mutuality and well-being' (Lawson 2007, 9). It also recognises how different historical and institutional relationships produce the need *for care*. Such a perspective can be transposed onto human-non-human relationships as well. In the context of the Anthropocene this includes how human decisions over time have created the conditions for unnatural disasters like arctic ice melt, drought, famine, flooding, mass extinction, etc. Depending on the particular need, care may also mean *retreat* from action.

The ethics of care is perhaps the most significant ethical theory to emerge from feminist analyses. How it translates into the world of security – so often filled with danger, harm, and violence – is an evolving, still unsettled question. Feminist security studies is a diverse and well-institutionalised sub-field, but the idea of care remains relatively under-developed as a security concept. When it has been examined, most notably over the past two decades by scholars like Sara Ruddick (1989), Fiona Robinson (1999, 2011), Virginia Held (2006), Kimberly Hutchings (1999; 2000; Hutchings and Frazer 2014) and Karin Fierke (2014; 2016) care ethics and security have coalesced around the connections between the universal and the particular. They argue against security logics that emphasise the ontological primacy of *homo economicus*: the concept of man as an independent, value-maximising and self-reliant subject. Such thinking obscures the particular social reality around the world, especially the experiences felt by women, who are more likely to 'define themselves in and through their relations with children and other family members— including those who are elderly or chronically ill—or with friends or members of their communities' (Robinson 2011, 90). More directly it helps maintain a deeply unjust and violent international society that views militarism as an inevitable byproduct of human nature rather than a masculinised ideology produced through social practice.

These care authors explore the contours of contemporary security issues like the concept of just war, humanitarian intervention, peacekeeping, and human security. Though each offers a unique position, a unifying thread has been a fixation on the practices rather than the principles that contribute to violence. Most crucially they emphasise the persistence of everyday material insecurities (Robinson 2016). Instead of strictly focusing on the spectacular moments of conflict and violence that accompany the breakdowns in social order, a feminist ethics of security also looks to 'marginalised sites' (Stern 2006, 182-183). Rather than the Schmittian inspired version of securitization that is enacted via the transition to a state of exception, care acknowledges the relentless insecurities of the unexceptional. The invocation of care also provides an alternative to the atomistic theories of ethical virtue that emphasise righteous, masculine qualities of honour, courage, intelligence, and detachment.

Toward a Security of Care

Can care, something we are told is ephemeral and localised, be considered an adequate response to Anthropocene threats that are planet-wide and occur along geological timescales? Can it truthfully be expected to transform human actions that are relentlessly critiqued as rapacious and self-interested? Will it stop the seemingly inevitable 'climate wars' (Dyer 2009; Parenti 2012)? What if it is used to legitimate neoliberal forms of 'humanitarianism' which are so often accompanied by sovereign and/or biopolitical violence on vulnerable populations (Piotukh 2015)? And just what can an ethos of care do to subvert or transform the power-laden carbon lock-ins found in technological, organizational, social and institutional systems (Unruh 2002)?

If held to such standards, the answer is, of course, to concede that care itself is inadequate. It will not on its own prevent the earth from warming, hinder the damaging powers of market processes, or overcome the deep divisions that separate humans from each other and from the wider webs of life in which we are all enmeshed. Yet part of the issue with answering the above charges is that the questions themselves are remnants of a past age, whereby security is a (human) good to be achieved through action. Care helps repurpose the pursuit of security in the Anthropocene – allowing for diverse ethical responses fixated on complex human and nonhuman relations - without simultaneously offering promise, emancipation, or a fixation on the tragic. Our Holocene-bred logics that champion reductive forms of safety and security are barriers to Anthropocene-era struggles which require a level of intellectual openness that expand and push the boundaries of comfort for most security scholars.

By activating multiple traditions of care, found often in subaltern discourses/ practices, we can recode and reclaim security away from its fatalistic determinism that dooms the world to apocalyptic conflicts over dwindling resources. Even if such a future comes to pass, the injunction to care is not diminished. Care allows us to cross the scalar and temporal zones that are impenetrable to conventional security studies, transcend the human-nature binaries that restrict who or what is worthy of ethical consideration, and make visible the immanent forms of relationality that bind us with our non-human companions. Given the character of Earth system changes care is appropriate because it demands nothing in return - no search for justice and reciprocity in a world that is often indifferent or openly hostile to us. If we are to take the Anthropocene seriously we need to grow accustomed to, in fact, embrace, loss and failure. It subverts the security problematique – the search for stasis, control, and predictability. A caring response obliges us to act in a spirit of empathy; to engage in gift-giving, to extend hospitality and kinship to human and non-human strangers; and to feel gratitude in the midst of ongoing, seemingly perpetual, social and ecological crises. This pushes us toward an affirmative sensibility that does not avoid pain, but helps us transcend,

> 'The resignation and passivity that ensue from being hurt, lost, and dispossessed. One has to become ethical, as opposed to applying moral rules and protocols as a form of self-protection. An adequate ethical relation is capable of sustaining the subject in his or her quest for more inter-relations with others, i.e., more 'Life', motion, change and transformation.' (Braidotti 2011, 289)

The appeal for care is of course open-ended and should not be considered definitive, even less a blueprint for action. All of these components depend upon the radical rethinking of subjectivity in security – from our ideas about the self-contained human as a security actor to the detached versions of nature that characterise so much security literature.

Care Sensibility in the Anthropocene

This final section will briefly touch on the ways that care can be enacted as a security sensibility in the Anthropocene. Principally, it helps us acknowledge new forms of risk, uncertainty, and failure. It also allows us to focus on the micropolitics of the self and community in relation to a widened circle of others without seeking justice or reciprocity.

It is now common to see suggestions that risk has become the dominant logic of security (Zedner 2009; O'Malley 2004). Olaf Corry explains that rather than defending against and deterring identifiable foes and criminals our security practices are designed around prevention, probabilities, possible future scenarios and managing diffuse risks (2012, 36). The new geological interval tells us to acknowledge and expect monumental changes, not just in terms of a warming climate, but also rising seas, a growing intensity of storm activities, increasing periods of extreme drought, and a mass extinction event not seen in 56 million years (Kolbert 2014). These changes are too severe and unpredictable to properly mitigate risk or assuage fears about the known and unknown impacts. Partially as a result there exists now a new primacy of risk as an operating principle as well as a suite of diverse characteristics we might call risk practices. Technology is partially responsible but so must we also focus on the shifting role of seemingly non-security actors, like the insurance industry, who are at the forefront of responding to global environmental change. Given the complexity and unpredictability of the Earth system risk comprises a key avenue where the Anthropocene and security meet.

In many ways a security of care allows us to embrace the diverse ways that risk and uncertainty intersect in the Anthropocene. To adopt a perspective of care would be to accept the fact that what the world will look like in fifty or a hundred or a thousand years is largely unknown yet these varying temporal scales are worthy of our attention. Though we cannot be certain in specific terms, we know that our climatic future will not resemble our past, and thus our expectations of security must also change, away from preparing for immediate, identifiable, and predicted 'foes' and towards a broader security ecology that understands that Anthropocene risk is inevitable and inherently relational. The speed and scale of global change in the Anthropocene is almost imponderable or unimaginable and demands care rather than fear or hope.

Extending care and promoting empathic relations in our security practices into security requires an awareness of entanglement and relationality. Widening the circle of security to encompass not just humans and states, but also the generations unborn, non-humans, and ecosystems, is the necessary first step that allows us to advance multi-sited forms of care. I say multi-sited because it would be ineffectual and contrary to its spirit to restrict care to state-based policies or to advocate for a retreat to inward-focused forms of self-care. Both of these have no chance, on their own, to secure the planet. In fact, the restriction of viable security actions to a single level would be unaligned with the distribution of the Anthropocene's security effects. The Anthropocene incorporates intertwined drivers, each with dispersed and unequal effects that cannot be easily separated.

Take for instance the growing use of nitrogen to fertilise food crops. The flows of biogeochemicals like nitrogen and phosphorous are used as one of the control variables that make up their planetary boundaries framework (Steffen et al. 2015). These identified thresholds are used to show the capacity of the Earth system to persist in a Holocene-like state. Crossing the planet's 'safe operating spaces' impacts the resilience of the system, leading eventually to global-level transitions. Nitrogen cycling has quite likely never been a topic that has interested security scholars. The growing availability of nitrogen, though, has been a major reason for the dramatic increase in food security for some countries and simultaneously posed increasing threats to human and ecosystem health. The world is at once too nitrogen-rich and nitrogen-poor. Embracing a caring sensibility in this instance would entail acknowledging nitrogen and other biogeochemical flows as Anthropocene security issues not by virtue of their potential to undermine global peace or community safety, but because they enact what Audra Mitchell terms 'worldly notions of harm', distributed across time, space, and worlds of being (Mitchell 2014). Certainly these flows affect the daily well-being of individuals (mostly in obtuse ways), but they also point to something more complex and ultimately unsettling; namely that security exists not as the liminal moment that divides safety from danger for a defined moral (human) community, but as a series of banal planetary functions made up of complex human and non-human assemblages.

The same experience can be applied to other markers of the Anthropocene – including the functioning of the oceans, climate change, or biosphere integrity. These are increasingly accepted as legitimate security concerns yet they are experienced narrowly, as glimpses that accord to dominant anthropocentric and instrumental abstractions. Using a sensibility of care, we might reverse this and give recognition to the complex, strange, and entangled natural entities rather than ignoring them or viewing them as adversaries, allies, or potential recipients of reciprocal forms of justice.

This can be pursued in a number of different ways. Conventionally it means amplifying by whatever means available the injunction to care for the vibrant and diverse security of earthly life that exists in relation to our own daily choices. According to William Connolly (2013, 131), the idea is to fold amplified versions of care into 'operational patterns of desire, faith, will, identity, and self-interest, rather than to rise to a disinterested level entirely above the mundane worlds of desire, instrumentality, and politics.' These patterns, which are already so prevalent in security thinking could be amended through cultivating micro-political interventions that can occur across individual and local scales to, for example, reflect on how food practices affect the efficiency of food systems and intersect with diverse forms of harm across lifeworlds. This could emphasise building the resilience of local food production by accepting lower yields in areas with high nitrogen pollution, while simultaneously increasing nitrogen use in sustainable ways in areas that are deprived (Biermann et al 2016).

Finally, sensibilities of care also attune us to indigenous ontologies that have long emphasised the entangled needs of humans and non-humans within interdependent communities. For millennia indigenous thinkers have constructed and passed down through generations, interpretations of sentient environments that are enacted by the complex and lively relationships between people and non-human presences, including the climate, ancestors, water, and spirits.[21] Take for instance the Tlatokan Atlahuak Declaration, from the Indigenous Peoples Parallel Forum of the Fourth World Water Forum in 2006, which claimed that, 'We have been placed upon this earth, each in our own traditional sacred land and territory to care for all of creation and water ... our traditional knowledge, laws and forms of life teach us to be responsible and caring for this sacred gift that connects all life' (Third World Water Forum, quoted in Powys Whye and Cuomo 2016). In these cases responsibility is not solely the domain of humans, but felt by other worlds of being too. Water is not inert but holds its own forcefulness. Deborah McGregor, an Anishinaabe scholar and activist explains:

> Water has a role and a responsibility to fulfill, just as people do. We do not have the right to interfere with water's duties to the rest of Creation. Indigenous knowledge tells us that water is the blood of Mother Earth and that water itself is considered a living entity with just as much right to live as we have. (McGregor 2009, 37–38, quoted in Powys Whyte and Cuomo 2016, 8.)

---

[21] It is important not to homogenise distinct indigenous voices and traditions and to acknowledge the diversity of thought present in indigenous literatures. Indigenous philosophy emphasises the importance of place in knowledge production and avoid essentialist conceptions of pan-Indigenous philosophy (Sundberg 2014)

On its face the Anthropocene is a simple, almost intuitive idea. Since our earliest days, humans have altered local environments (Barnosky 2008). Yet, the Anthropocene is different. Of course it is monstrous in terms of its material consequences. On this alone, our understandings of security are challenged. Additionally, the Anthropocene concept compels us to acknowledge how security interacts with diverse lifeworlds that exist within, above, below, and around humans, acting in ways both pacific and threatening. Responding to this entails significant alterations to our security logics. This article argued that a care sensibility, one that is immeasurably old and yet fluid enough to adapt to our new world, can help us respond to the seemingly inescapable limits of planetary security despite the absence of any promise of reciprocity.

References

Barnosky, Anthony D., 2008. "Megafauna biomass tradeoff as a driver of Quaternary and Future Extinctions." *Proceedings of National Academy of Science of the United States of America* 105 (1): 11543-11548.

Biermann Frank, Xuemei Bai, Ninad Bondre, Wendy Broadgate, Chen-Tung Arthur Chen, Opha Pauline Dube, Jan Willem Erisman, Marion Glaser, Sandra Van der Hel, Maria Carmen Lemos, Sybil Seitzinger, and Karen C. Seto. 2016. "Down to Earth: Contextualising the Anthropocene." *Global Environmental Change* 39: 341-350.

Braidotti, Rosi. 2011. *Nomadic Theory: The Portable Rosi Braidotti*. New York: Columbia University Press.

Burke Anthony, Stefanie Fishel, Audra Mitchell, Simon Dalby, and Daniel Levine. 2016. "Planet Politics A Manifesto from the End of IR." *Millennium: Journal of International Studies* 44 (3): 499-523.

Clark, Nigel. 2016. "Anthropocene Incitements: Toward a Politics and Ethics of Ex- orbitant Planetarity." In *The Politics of Globality Since 1945*, edited by Rens van Munster and Casper Sylvest, 126-146. Milton Park: Routledge.

Collins, Stephanie. 2015. *The Core of Care Ethics*. New York, NY: Palgrave Macmillan.

Connolly, William E., 2013. *The Fragility of Things*. Durham: Duke University Press.

Corry, Olaf. 2012. "Risk Securitisation and 'Riskification': Second-order

Security and the Politics of Climate Change." *Millennium: Journal of International Studies* 40 (2): 235-258.

Dyer, Gwynne. 2009. *Climate Wars*. Toronto: Vintage Canada.

Engster, Daniel. 2004. "Care Ethics and Natural Law Theory: Toward an Institutional Political Theory of Caring." *The Journal of Politics* 66 (2): 113:135.

Fierke, Karin. 2014. "Who is My Neighbour? Memories of the Holocaust/*al Nakba* and a Global Ethic of Care." *European Journal of International Relations* 20 (3):787-209.

Fierke, Karin. 2016. "Security as Ethics: An Orthogonal Rotation from Egoism to Compassion. In *Ethical Security Studies: A New Research Agenda*, edited by Jonna Nyman and Anthony Burke, 116-131. Milton Park: Routledge.

Hamilton, John T., 2013. *Security, Politics, Humanity, and the Philology of Care*. Princeton N.J.: Princeton University Press.

Harrington, Cameron. 2016. "The Ends of the World: International Relations and The Anthropocene." 44 (3): 478-498.

Heidegger, Martin. 1978 [1962]. *Being and Time*. Translated by John Macquarrie and Edward Robinson. Oxford, UK: Wiley-Blackwell.

Held, Virginia. 2006. *The Ethics of Care: Personal, Political and Global*. Oxford: Oxford University Press.

Hutchings, Kimberly. 2000. "Towards a Feminist International Ethics." *Review of International Studies* 26: 111-130.

Hutchings, Kimberly. 1999. *International Political Theory: Re-thinking Ethics in a Global Era*. London: Sage.

Hutchings, Kimberly, and Elizabeth Frazer. 2014. "Revisiting Ruddick: Feminism, Pacifism and Non-Violence." *Journal of International Political Theory* 10 (1): 109   -124.

Kolbert, Elizabeth. 2014. *The Sixth Extinction: An Unnatural History.* New York: Henry Holt and Company, 2014.

Latour, Bruno. 2011. "Waiting for Gaia. Composing the Common World through Arts and Politics." Lecture at the French Institute, London, November 2011.

Lawson, Victoria. 2007. "Geographies of Care and Responsibility." *Annals of the Association of American Geographers*. 97 (1): 1-11.

Mitchell, Audra, 2014. "Only Human? A Worldly Approach to Security." *Security Dialogue* 45 (1): 5–21

O'Malley, Pat. 2004. *Risk, Uncertainty, and Government*. London: The GlassHouse Press.

Parenti, Christian. 2012. *Tropic of Chaos: Climate Change and the New Geography of Violence*. New York: Nation Books.

Piotukh, Volha. 2015. *Biopolitics, Governmentality and Humanitarianism: 'Caring' for the Population in Afghanistan and Belarus*. Milton Park: Routledge.

Plumwood, Val. 2002. *Environmental Culture: The Ecological Crisis of Reason*. London and New York: Routledge.

Population Reference Bureau. 2016. "2016 World Population Sheet." Accessed November 9, 2016. http://www.prb.org/Publications/ DataSheets/2016/2016-world-population-data-sheet.aspx

Powys Whyte, Kyle, and Chris Cuomo. 2016. "Ethics of Caring in Environmental Ethics: Indigenous and Feminist Philosophies." In *The Oxford Handbook of Environmental Ethics*, edited by Stephen M. Gardiner and Allen Thompson. New York: Oxford University Press.

Robinson, Fiona. 1999. *Globalising Care: Ethics, Feminist Theory, and International Relations*. Boulder, CO: Westview Press.

Robinson, Fiona. 2011. *The ethics of care: A Feminist Approach to Human Security*. Philadelphia: Temple University Press.

Robinson, Fiona. 2016. "Feminist Care Ethics and Everyday Insecurities." In *Ethical Security Studies: A New Research Agenda*, edited by Jonna Nyman and Anthony Burke, 116-131. Milton Park: Routledge.

Ruddick, Sara. 1989. *Maternal Thinking: Toward a Politics of Peace*. Boston: Beacon Press.

Serres, Michael. 1995. *The Natural Contract*. Translated by Elizabeth MacArthur and William Paulson. Ann Arbor: University of Michigan Press.

Steffen, Will et al. 2015. "Planetary Boundaries: Guiding Human Development on a Changing Planet." *Science* 347 (6233): 736-748.

Stern, Maria. 2006. "Racism, Sexism, Classism and Much More: Reading Security-Identity in Marginalised Sites." In *Feminist Methods in International Relations*, edited by, Brooke Eckersley, Maria Stern and Jacqui True, 174-197. Cambridge: Cambridge University Press:

Sundberg, Juanita. 2014. "Decolonising Posthumanist Geographies." *Cultural Geographies* 21 (1): 33-47.

Unruh, Gregory C., 2002. "Escaping Carbon Lock-In." *Energy Policy* 30 (4): 317-325.

Walker, R. B. J., 1993. *Inside/Outside: International Relations as Political Theory.* Cambridge: Cambridge University Press.

Zedner, Lucia. 2009. *Security*. New York: Routledge.

8

Global Security in a Posthuman Age? IR and the Anthropocene Challenge

DELF ROTHE

We have entered the age of the Anthropocene – a new geological epoch, which is defined by the human impact on planet Earth (Crutzen 2002; Steffen, Crutzen and McNeill and Steffen 2007; Zalasiewicz et al. 2011). This claim, initially made by geochemist and Nobel Prize laureate Paul Crutzen and popularised by several geologists and Earth scientists, is currently gaining traction in the critical literature in International Relations (IR). Drawing upon the reception of the Anthropocene concept by posthumanist or new materialist thinkers like Bruno Latour (2012; 2015) or Donna Haraway (2015), an increasing number of scholars are challenging established ontological concepts in IR, including geopolitics, security, or global governance (Dalby 2013a; Fagan 2016; Harrington 2016; Harrington and Shearing 2016; Mayer and Schouten 2012; Mitchell 2014). Others even go so far as to announce the end of IR as a discipline (Agathangelou 2016, 330), which would be '[...] undone by the reality of the planet' (Burke et al. 2016, 501).

The existing IR literature on the Anthropocene takes the fact that humanity has become a telluric force like volcanism or tectonic plate movements as proof of a fundamental ontological flaw in dominant IR theories and concepts, i.e. the 'bifurcation of nature' (Latour 2015). A flawed distinction between the natural and the social worlds would, according to this critique, characterise all major IR theories (see e.g. Harrington in this volume; McDonald in this volume). The Anthropocene would instead prove that a clear distinction between nature and culture, between subject and object cannot be drawn. In the Anthropocene, the planet is actively interfering in human affairs, while humans at the same time have begun to transform the planet (Yusoff 2013,

2806). Classical approaches of geopolitics that would take the Earth (geo) as the stable environment, in which global power politics unfolds, would become inappropriate (Dalby 2013b, 39-40). Mainstream approaches of security would be equally problematic in the Anthropocene epoch. The very idea of a state securing its own territory from external threats or protecting its population from the contingencies of life (such as natural disasters, or diseases, etc.) is predicated upon 'the separation of the human from an external nature' (Fagan 2016, 8). Yet, even the critical literature on environmental or human security is accused of being guilty of reproducing the artificial divide between the natural and social worlds (Fagan 2016, 14-16). Either 'the environment' would be constructed as a referent object endangered by human activity or human communities would vice versa be portrayed as threatened by some external nature. Opposing these established concepts and theories, the Anthropocene literature holds that 'modern assumptions of nature as separate from humanity have never been accurate. The biosphere is a hybrid of the artificial and the natural' (Dalby 2013b, 40). Drawing on these theoretical reflections, the IR Anthropocene literature calls for a fundamental rethinking of security in terms of a 'worldly approach to security' (Mitchell 2014), 'ecosystem resilience' (McDonald in this volume), or security as an 'ethos of care' (Harrington in this volume).

From a different angle, a redefinition of security in posthumanist terms has been less welcomed. By proving the nature/culture divide – which is at the heart of the liberal enlightenment project – wrong, the Anthropocene literature would also do away with liberal aspirations of progress and promises of protection (Chandler 2013; Grove and Chandler 2016; Vrasti and Michelsen 2016). Instead, the Anthropocene concept would promote a mere politics of adaptation and resilience, a form of post-politics, in which humans stop seeking transformation of their living conditions and instead accept their embeddeddness into fragile and crisis-prone socio-ecological systems (Evans and Reid 2014). In the age of the Anthropocene, it is argued, 'The classic quest after the "good life", once a starting point for both an art of living and the art of governing, is replaced by the more minimalist, almost realpolitik, striving for adaptive survival' (Vrasti and Michelsen 2016, 4).

In this contribution, I argue that both lines of argument – the affirmative and the critical literature on posthuman security in the Anthropocene – suffer from two related shortcomings. First, I hold that while the IR debate on the Anthropocene is strongly influenced by different strands of posthumanist and new materialist thought, the different theoretical traditions within this field and their implications for the understanding of the Anthropocene are seldom reflected. Posthumanism/new materialism has become a catchall term to denote any approach rejecting the nature/culture divide, including Actor-Network-Theory (ANT), Object-Oriented-Ontology (OOO), vital materialism, or critical posthumanism (see Kaltofen in this volume). This is problematic because, despite their common commitment to a post-Cartesian ontology, these approaches have quite distinct philosophical backgrounds and thus different ontological, epistemological and methodological implications (see also Cudworth and Hobden 2015). Second, in both the affirmative and the critical take on posthuman notions of security, the 'advent of the Anthropocene' (Hamilton et al., 5) and the assumption that it represents a fundamental rupture of our established anthropocentric theoretical concepts is simply taken for granted. In both literatures, there seems to be no doubt that we have entered a 'posthuman age' (Braidotti 2016, 33; Ferrando 2013, 32). Thereby, the literature gives the impression that we would exactly know what this 'new reality of the Anthropocene' (McDonald in this volume) is and presents it as a single truth (a post-anthropocentric/post-humanist age) with a single set of normative implications: 'The Anthropocene signals both the end of nature and the end of humanism' (Grove and Chandler 2016, 6).

In this contribution, I seek to sketch an alternative, sociological, account of security in the Anthropocene. This alternative approach starts from the assumption that the planetary crisis that we call the Anthropocene is inaccessible and withdrawn. Hence, an incredible amount of labour is required to render it visible and thinkable in the first place. My approach thus seeks to trace and map the assemblages or actor-networks, in which traces of the Anthropocene and resulting security risks become enacted through a multiplicity of practices and technologies (see also Rothe 2017). To develop this approach, the contribution starts by introducing and discussing two competing approaches that are often lumped together under the label of new materialism but in fact provide two almost oppositional perspectives on the question of how we can know the Anthropocene: ANT and OOO. In the third section, these two perspectives on the Anthropocene are related to the debate on Anthropocene security in IR. The fourth section sketches the contours of a sociological variant of Anthropocene security as alternative to the existing philosophical version that dominates the current debate in critical IR.

New Materialism between Object-Oriented-Ontology and Actor-Network-Theory

The accounts of new materialism and posthumanism in recent debates on security in International Relations are painted with a very broad brush stroke. Labels such as the 'new material turn' or the 'posthuman turn' are used to refer to a whole range of different theories from different disciplinary contexts and philosophical traditions, which sometimes even contradict each other. The only common ground of these heterogeneous approaches is the rejection of anthropocentrism and a Cartesian worldview (see also Cudworth and Hobden 2015, 141; Kaltofen in this volume). In the following, I want to illustrate this claim by discussing and comparing two prominent approaches that are often lumped together under the label of new materialism but draw upon almost oppositional theoretical assumptions: Object-Oriented-Ontology (OOO) and Actor-Network-Theory (ANT).

In the critical security literature, Object-Oriented-ontology (OOO) is quite often used synonymously to the broader label of 'new materialism.' In this perspective, OOO is equated with an approach of '[...] imagining the world from the view point of objects' (Kaltofen in this volume). However, this narrow understanding of OOO ignores the philosophical implications that come along with the approach. For, OOOs proposition is not merely that we 'need to stop trying to understand the world in terms of subject-object relations' (Kaltofen in this volume). Rather, its point is to stop thinking of the world in relational ways in general: 'It is necessary to staunchly defend the autonomy of objects or substances, refusing any reduction of objects to their relations, whether these relations be relations to humans or other objects' (Bryant 2011, 26). For OOO, there is a virtual inner essence of things – an ontological surplus that is never completely actualised in an object's relations to other objects. In OOO's terms, this inner core can neither be perceived by human subjects nor by other objects with which they interact – objects are 'withdrawn' (Bryant 2011, 26-31; Harman 2005). Here, OOO resembles the structuralist psychoanalysis of Jacques Lacan and his notion of the subject as 'void' (Žižek 2016, 66-69). For Lacan, the subject is never fully actualised – it is marked by a fundamental lack of identity, which can never be closed. For OOO 'all objects are akin to Lacanian divided subjects' (Žižek 2016, 69): objects are divided between their actual qualities in networks and their virtual inner core that only exists as potentiality but is never fully actualised. Thus, contingency is not just an epistemological problem – as a human incapability to grasp a complex reality, which is fully constituted – but an essentially ontological feature of objects themselves.

OOO, with its 'deeply non-relational conception of the reality of things' (Bennett 2012, 226), needs to be distinguished from relational 'materialist' theories such as ANT (see also Žižek 2016). In the IR literature ANT has been widely received in critical security works on security technologies such as drones, border control technologies, or algorithmic surveillance (see Kaltofen in this volume). Understood as an empirical version of poststructuralism – or as 'material semiotics' (Law 2009, 145-146) – ANT transfers the semiotic idea of the relational constitution of meaning to the material world. Challenging the classical semiotic distinction between the signifier and the signified it holds that any sign has a material dimension and any thing in the world is itself a sign. Things in the world receive their identity and meaning through their associative relations to other elements in complex and fluid assemblages, or actor-networks (Latour 2005; Law 1999). Instead of viewing texts, images and other semiotic systems as representations of a pre-existing single reality, ANT shows how the interplay of expert practices, scientific discourses, technologies, and visuals constitute *multiple realities* (Hind and Lammes 2016, 81-82). According to ANT-scholar Annemarie Mol, ontology 'is not given in the order of things but [...] ontologies are brought into being, sustained, or allowed to wither away in common, day-to-day, sociomaterial practices' (Mol 2002, 6). Agency, in this understanding, is not linked to notions of human will or intention but is distributed across the human and non-human elements of actor-networks. Agency thus rests in the capability of making-a-difference in the world (Latour 2005).

The crucial ontological differences between ANT and OOO are seldom acknowledged in the IR literature. OOO holds that objects are non-relational, withdrawn, and marked by their potentiality to be otherwise. For ANT, on the contrary, any thing in the world is real – and only real – insofar as it acts upon other things (Harman 2015). This is an ontology of pure immanence, in which things in the world are relationally constituted in situated practices.

The described theoretical differences have important methodological implications. From an OOO perspective, the virtual inner core of objects – a potentiality that is never fully actualized – is not observable through the researcher. This assumption adds practices of speculation, mythical storytelling, practices of imagination and art as important ingredients of our endeavours to make sense of a phenomenon like the Anthropocene (Bryant, Srnicek and Harman 2011; Morton 2013). For ANT, on the contrary, the power of things rests in their ability to establish associative relations between heretofore unrelated phenomena (Cudworth and Hobden 2015, 444). A new technology such as a microscope or a satellite might enable novel ways of seeing the world, or altering the space-time of actor-networks thereby creating new affective relations between heretofore unrelated phenomena – e.g. between researchers and microbes. The core methodological position of ANT thus is empiricism (see Koddenbrock 2015). Careful participant observation – or the study of archives and secondary literature – is required to trace and study the relations of humans, non-humans, technologies, and discourses in situated practices and show how they relationally afford each other with identity and meaning.

Security in the Anthropocene: Between Hyperobjects and Actor-networks

At the heart of the existing IR literature on security in the Anthropocene are two arguments: first, with the advent of the Anthropocene we are entering a new planetary reality, in which conditions of (human and non-human) life become radically altered and threatened (Burke et al. 2016, 506; Harrington 2016, 481-482). Second, this new reality finally proves the inappropriateness of our theoretical conceptions and political institutions that were built for the Holocene and that drew upon a clear divide between the human and the natural world (Burke et al. 2016, 510; Fagan 2016, 13). This literature holds that the Anthropocene is more than a scientific (i.e. geological) concept. So, it is not simply a discursive or mental construction but has a material dimension and refers to a certain planetary reality (Harrington 2016, 482). I would agree. But what kind of thing (or object), then, is the Anthropocene exactly? How can we actually know it (and who is 'we')? What does it mean to be 'in' the Anthropocene? I would argue that these fundamental questions have been skipped in the unfolding IR literature on the Anthropocene.

I seek answers to these unasked questions from the perspective of the two theoretical approaches briefly described in the previous section. To address these questions from the perspective of OOO, it is helpful to take a closer look at Timothy Morton's recent work on hyperobjects (Morton 2013). Morton transfers the ideas of OOO to the realm of ecology and tries to answer the question of how to make sense of complex and unruly objects like climate change. He proposes the notion of hyperobjects to refer to these objects, which are so widely distributed in time and space that they are omnipresent – i.e. it is not possible to escape them – but at the same time absent and withdrawn – in the sense that they elude perception and cognition (Morton 2013, 1-3). According to Morton, hyperobjects, such as climate change, are interobjective, as they are constituted by the relations of several objects. Furthermore, they are nonlocal: while hyperobjects have concrete local impacts, their totality does never materialise locally (Morton 2013, 38). Thus, other objects (including humans) can experience hyperobjects only indirectly (for example, climate change can be experienced via local impacts or as rising ocean levels). Due to these characteristics, there will never be absolute scientific certainty about their existence. Thus, quite paradoxically, at a point of time when the impacts of climate change are being felt at more and more places in the world, also the amount of climate skepticism and denial is rising.

The Anthropocene, then, could be understood as an epoch, which is marked by the rise of hyperobjects – or even as a meta-hyperobject, which is itself constituted by the interrelation of several hyperobjects including climate change, nuclear power, etc. The Anthropocene is thus equally totalising and withdrawn: the Anthropocene is a new planetary real – a state-shift of the entire Earth System that cannot be known or sensed directly and can hence only be addressed indirectly. It is thus no surprise that a whole range of *art projects* are emerging that try to capture the spectral phenomenon of the

Anthropocene in artefacts and artworks; and that the humanities are turning towards indigenous sources of spiritual and mythical knowledge to make sense of this new planetary real. If the Anthropocene is the age of hyperobjects that are unthinkable and withdrawn '[...] we need some other basis for making decisions about a future to which we have no real sense of connection' (Morton 2010). Such a perspective is very much in line with the dominant reception of the Anthropocene in IR/Critical Security Studies. Here, the Anthropocene takes the form of a new planetary real – a dislocative moment that crucially challenges our established concepts and world views. This literature identifies 'alternative' sources of knowledge, for example in spiritual, indigenous (i.e. premodern) conceptions of the world (see Mitchell in this volume).

What this perspective ignores, however, is the incredible amount of labour required to render the Anthropocene's traces visible and sizable in the first place (Wark 2015a). For, as Slavoj Zizek reminds us '[...] We do not only miss an appropriate language but also an approbative sensation-experience of this world' (Žižek 2016, 44) I am following here McKenzie Wark (2014), who points to the vast posthuman assemblage of satellites, weather stations, computer simulations, researchers, mechanisms of international cooperation, which renders hyperobjects like climate change visible, sizable or calculable in the first place (see Edwards 2010; Wark 2015b, 166-182). This is where we (re-)enter ANT turf: unlike for OOO, for Latour and other ANT scholars, Gaia does not exist until it becomes woven into our conception of the world (Harman 2015). To become 'matter-real' and 'matter-ing' (Moser 2008, 99) the Anthropocene needs to be enacted by complex actor-networks of planetary dimensions: scientific practices and technologies such as satellite earth observation or stratigraphic research render the material traces of the Anthropocene visible (van Munster and Sylvest 2016, 4-10). Discursive and aesthetic practices of scientists, writers, activists and artists weave these traces into broader meaningful narratives of the Earth — or 'geostories' (Bonneuil 2015, 17).

I would thus follow Sam Randalls (2015) who argues that 'the Anthropo(s) cene is thoroughly multiple.' This implies that competing versions of the Anthropocene exist, each accompanied with a different set of policy and ethical conclusions. This is my main point of critique of the existing IR literature on security in the Anthropocene: it takes the Anthropocene as a fixed and given phenomenon, which is used to develop a single set of normative arguments about the redefinition of core concepts in IR like security or geopolitics.

Just as Wark (2015a) claims that OOO 'occludes the ways in which objects are known in the first place,' the IR literature on the Anthropocene occludes the ways in which the Anthropocene can be known. Wark holds that this 'mystification' is unfolding in three steps: firstly, knowledge of an object is produced by a whole range of human and non-human practices; secondly, these practices are generalised in the form of images and metaphors; thirdly, the original labour that was required to construct these metaphors is erased: 'the metaphor will then be claimed to be what precedes all those other steps when it is actually a later derivation' (Wark 2015a). In the IR literature on the Anthropocene, the same happens: the Anthropocene becomes an abstracted imagery, a massive metaphor, in which all the labour required to produce it in the first place becomes black-boxed. The image of the Anthropocene is then taken as evidence of the hubris of our discipline as well as previous human attempts to deal with the climate crisis. For example, Harrington (2016, 479) proposes to understand the Anthropocene as a new defining marker of IR. However, as the heated debate on the start date of the Anthropocene in Geology and the Earth Sciences reminds us, we might have been in the Anthropocene for several hundreds or even thousands of years – so, how can this epoch reasonably represent a temporal marker for IR? The deployment of the Anthropocene as a metaphor becomes apparent in the ambiguous ways, in which the term Anthropocene is deployed: The notions of 'the Anthropocene,' 'the Anthropocene concept' or the 'Anthropocene imaginary' are used alternatively – sometimes within one and the same article (Grove and Chandler 2016, 1-4). So, it becomes unclear what actually challenges our conceptions of the world: is it the Anthropocene itself (but how do we know this withdrawn thing?), or some of its more visible footprints and traces (but how are these becoming visible in the first place)? Or is it a certain discourse, concept or imaginary is challenging our human hubris?

Towards a Sociological Variant of Anthropocene Security

I want to use the remainder of this contribution to make a proposal for an alternative version of security in the Anthropocene. Firstly, rather than taking the Anthropocene and its security implications as a given starting point of a theoretical/philosophical discussion of security, this alternative version addresses the Anthropocene as an open question. It stresses the unknowability of the Anthropocene (and its security implications) and the incredible amount of labour and practice required to render it intelligible. Instead of discussing the question of how security in the Anthropocene should look like, such an approach asks how security practices in the Anthropocene actually look like. Identifying itself as a sociological version of Anthropocene security, the approach holds that neither do security risks in the Anthropocene simply exist out there, nor are they reducible to mere discursive constructions or mental concepts. Rather, they become 'matter-real' through a whole multiplicity of practices in socio-technological networks. These comprise remote sensors, computing power, simulation models, media, researchers, and many other things that together render traces of the Anthropocene and their security implications visible (Edwards 2010; McQuillan 2016; van Munster and Sylvest 2016). Such risks become 'matter-real' as computer models, risk maps, statistical probabilities, satellite images, future scenarios, or colourful data visualizations (Jasanoff 2004; Schneider and Nocke 2014). The approach thus holds that the technosphere – just like the geosphere, biosphere or the hydrosphere – is part of the Anthropocene and that forms of securing in the Anthropocene are inherently digital (HKW 2016). It seeks to trace and map the actor-networks that emerge through the increasing cooperation of security officials, environmental researchers, NGOs strategic think-tanks, technology and data start-ups around concepts such as complexity, resilience, or big data.

Secondly, I agree with Sam Randalls (2015, 330) that the Anthropocene is always multiple and thus '[...] should not be taken to inspire a singular scientific, political or ethical view.' Exactly this is happening in the existing literature on security in the Anthropocene, which holds that the Anthropocene forces us to rethink our core concepts and institutions of security. Here, it often appears as if the overcoming of the nature/culture divide would already be a political act. Accepting our embeddeddness within the Earth System would allow for the development of a new sensitivity for our non-human co-inhabitants on this planet (see Grove and Chandler 2016, 7). By turning a vitalist materialist or posthumanist ontology into a political project one, however, risks re-essentialising the carefully deconstructed nature/culture divide (Luke 2016, 7). The Anthropocene, then, risks becoming another version of 'green ideology' (Stavrakakis 1997), in which 'the environment' as a core nodal point is replaced with Gaia or the Earth System. Similar to earlier forms of green ideology, posthuman conceptions of security in the IR literature carry the promise of a certain fullness-to-come once the human subject becomes fully embedded into and immersed within the socio-ecological Earth System (or local socio-ecological systems).

Starting from the notion of *multiple Anthropocenes*, on the contrary, I would propose a more empirical approach that describes the different security projects in the Anthropocene, each dealing with different security threats and governance problems, and unfolding within different social/ecological/technical assemblages. For example, a particularly prominent version of the Anthropocene understands it in (post-) apocalyptical terms (Bonneuil 2015, 27-28) as 'disaster to end all disasters' (Clark 2014, 21). Linking up with earlier forms of environmental eschatology, and organised around prominent boundary objects such as the 'planetary boundaries' concept (Steffen et al. 2015) such imaginaries help reinforce post-political forms of governance around the notion of resilience. In line with Lovelock's prediction of the 'revenge of Gaia' (Lovelock 2006), the planet here becomes enacted as a pathological Earth – a disequilibrium stage of the Earth System, posing non-linear and unpredictable risks for life on the planet (Grove and Chandler 2016, 7). As shocks, disasters or catastrophes can never be ruled-out, the lesson is that the socio-ecological systems at risk must become resilient themselves (Evans and Reid 2014). In other actor-networks Gaia becomes instead enacted as an enormous laboratory available for human experimentation and control. Post-environmentalists such as the members of the Californian Breakthrough Institute are dreaming of a future, in which humans self-consciously acknowledge their agency as a geological force and – 'as pilots of a hybrid techno-nature' (Bonneuil 2015, 25) – begin steering spaceship Earth into desired directions. Numerous research projects on different types of geoengineering all around the world are already exploring the options for intentional modifications of the Earth System (Yusoff, 2013). At the same time, businesses and government projects are increasingly trying to harness the power of technologies such as big data, artificial intelligence, smart devices and the internet of things for *ecological modernization* projects (Luke 2016, 10).

Thirdly, I want to make an argument against the aspiration to fully overcome the subject/object divide (Chagani 2014; see also Mitchell in this volume). The existing literature on security in the Anthropocene seems to imply that there is no alternative between the Cartesian ideal of a fully constituted, self-conscious human subject, on the one hand, and a completely flat ontology, in which no distinction between subject and object exists, on the other. Following David Howarth (2013) and Slavoj Žižek (2016) I want to argue that there is in fact the possibility of a 'third way' between these two extreme positions. This third way does not understand the subject as the fully constituted self-conscious human being that Descartes had described. Instead, subjectivity refers to a form of self-identity that is marked by a constitutive lack-of-fullness. The subject is a void in the signifying structure – a form of self-identity that is entirely relational depending on the symbolic structure into which it is thrown (Howarth 2013, 158; Žižek 2016, 58-59). Subjectivity, then, is not reserved to human individuals, but can as well refer to collective forms of identity that include both human and non-human elements. Following this interpretation, the Anthropocene could indeed become a crucial moment of dislocation that might be turned into radical forms of political agency and mobilised for a reconceptualization of our very concepts of security and politics. Yet, for this, we need to preserve the idea of political subjectivity. For, it can only be a political project that involves human actors, that could develop a vision of an alternative post-capitalist future around a set of core political demands and build a coalition of human and non-human members powerful enough to challenge the existing hegemony of global carboniferous capitalism and the discourses and practices of security that help sustain it.

References

Agathangelou, Anna M., 2016. "Bruno Latour and Ecology Politics: Poetics of Failure and Denial in IR." *Millennium* 44(3): 321-347.

Bennett, Jane. 2012. "Systems and Things: A Response to Graham Harman and Timothy Morton." *New Literary History* 43(2): 225-233.

Bonneuil, Christophe. 2015. "The Geological Turn: Narratives of the Anthropocene." In *The Anthropocene and The Global Environment Crisis: Rethinking Modernity in a New Epoch,* edited Hamilton, C., Gemenne, F. and Bonneuil, C. 17-83. Abingdon/New York: Routledge.

Braidotti, Rosi. 2016. "Jenseits des Menschen: Posthumanismus." *Aus Politik und Zeitgeschichte* 66: 33-38.

Bryant Levi, Nick Srnicek, and Graham Harman. 2010. "Towards a Speculative Philosophy." In *The Speculative Turn: Continental Materialism and Realism,* edited by Levi Bryant, Nick Srnicek, and Graham Harman, 1-19. Victoria, Australia: re.press.

Bryant, Levi. 2011. *The Democracy of Objects*. Chicago: Open Humanities Press.

Burke, Anthony, Stefanie Fishel, Audra Mitchell, Simon Dalby, and Daniel J. Levine. 2016. *"*Planet Politics: *A Manifesto from the End of IR.*" *Millennium Journal of International Studies* 44(3): 499–523.

Chagani, Fayaz. 2014. "Critical Political Ecology and the Seductions of Posthumanism." *Journal of Political Ecology* 21: 424-436.

Chandler, David. 2013. "The World of Attachment? The Post-humanist Challenge to Freedom and Necessity". *Millennium* 41(3): 516-534.

Clark, Nigel. 2014. "Geo-Politics and the Disaster of the Anthropocene." *The Sociological Review* 62(S1):19-37.

Crutzen, Paul J., 2002. "Geology of Mankind". *Nature* 415 (6867): 23-23.

Cudworth, Erika, and Stephen Hobden. 2015. "Liberation for Straw Dogs? Old Materialism, New Materialism, and The Challenge of an Emancipatory Posthumanism." *Globalizations* 12(1): 134-148.

Dalby, Simon. 2013a. "Biopolitics and Climate Security in the Anthropocene." *Geoforum* 49:184-192.

Dalby, Simon. 2013b. "The Geopolitics of Climate Change." *Political Geography* 37: 38-47.

Edwards, Paul N., 2010. *A Vast Machine: Computer Models, Climate Data, and The Politics of Global Warming.* Cambridge, MA: MIT Press.

Evans, Brad, and Julian Reid. 2014. *Resilient life: The Art of Living Dangerously.* Boston: John Wiley and Sons.

Fagan, Madeleine. 2016. "Security in the Anthropocene: Environment, Ecology, Escape." *European Journal of International Relations.*

Ferrando, Francesca. 2013. "Posthumanism, Transhumanism, Antihumanism, Metahumanism, and New Materialisms." *Existenz* 8(2): 26-32.

Grove, Kevin and David Chandler. 2016. "Introduction: Resilience and the Anthropocene: The Stakes of 'Renaturalising' Politics. Resilience." *International Policies, Practices and Discourses.* 1-13.

Haraway, Donna. 2015. "Anthropocene, Capitalocene, Plantationocene, Chthulucene: Making Kin." *Environmental Humanities* 6 (1): 159-165.

Harman, Graham. 2005. *Guerrilla metaphysics: Phenomenology and The Carpentry of Things.* Chicago: Open Court Publishing.

Harman, Graham. 2011. "On the Undermining of Objects Grant, Bruno, and Radical Philosophy." *In The Speculative Turn: Continental Materialism and Realism,* 21-40. Victoria: re.press.

Harman, Graham. 2015. "Morton's Hyperobjects and the Anthropocene." Talk at 26 Samfundshuset Kirkenes, Kirkenes, Norway, 26 November 2015. Online video available at https://vimeo.com/153480982 (accessed 21 December 2016).

Harrington, Cameron. 2016. "The Ends of the World: International Relations and the Anthropocene." *Millennium* 44 (3): 478-498.

Harrington, Cameron, and Clifford Shearing. 2016. *Security in the Anthropocene: Reflections on Safety and Care.* Bielefeld: Transcript.

Hind, Sam, and Sybille Lammes. 2016. "Digital Mapping as Double-Tap: Cartographic Modes, Calculations and Failures." *Global Discourse* 6 (1-2): 79-97.

HKW Haus der Kulturen der Welt 2016. "Anthropocene Curriculum Campus: The Technosphere Issue." Report: Session 'Sensing the Insensible', Available at: https://www.hkw.de/en/app/mediathek/video/50658 (accessed 4 January 2017).

Howarth, David R., 2013. *Poststructuralism and After: Structure, Subjectivity and Power.* Basingstoke and New York: Palgrave Macmillan.

Jasanoff, Sheila. 2004. "Heaven and Earth: The Politics of Environmental Images." In *Earthly Politics, Local and Global in Environmental Governance,* edited by Jasanoff, S. and Martello, M.L., 31-52. Boston: MIT Press.

Koddenbrock, Kai Jonas. 2015. "Strategies of Critique in International Relations: From Foucault and Latour towards Marx." *European Journal of International Relations* 21(2): 243–266.

Latour, Bruno. 2005. *Reassembling the Social: An introduction to Actor-Network-Theory.* Oxford: Oxford University Press, USA.

The Breakthrough. 2012. "Love Your Monsters: Why We Must Care for Our Technologies As We Do Our Children." Accessed January 5, 2017. http://thebreakthrough.org/index.php/journal/past-issues/issue-2/love-your-monsters

Latour, Bruno. 2015. "Telling Friends from Foes at the Time of the Anthropocene." In *The Anthropocene and The Global Environmental Crisis: Rethinking Modernity in a New Epoch,* edited by Hamilton, C., Gemenne, F. and Bonneuil, C, 145-155. New York: Routledge.

Law, John. 1999. "After ANT: Complexity, Naming and Topology." *The Sociological Review* 47(S1): 1-14.

Law, John. 2009. "Actor Network Theory and Material Semiotics" In *The new Blackwell companion to social theory*. 141-158. Malden, MA and Oxford: Blackwell.

Lovelock, James. 2006. *The Revenge of Gaia: Earth's Climate Crisis and the Future of Humanity.* New York: Basic Books.

Luke, Timothy W., 2016. "Reconstructing Social Theory and the Anthropocene." *European Journal of Social Theory* 20(1):80-94.

Mayer, Maximilian, and Peer Schouten. 2012. "Energy Security and Climate Security Under Conditions of the Anthropocene." In *Energy Security in the Era of Climate Change: The Asia-Pacific Experience*, edited by Luca Anceschi, and Jonathan Symons, 13-35. London: Palgrave Macmillan UK.

McQuillan, Dan. 2016. "The Anthropocene, Resilience and Post-Colonial Computation." *Resilience: International Policies, Practices and Discourses* 1-18.

Mitchell, Audra. 2014. "Only human? A Worldly Approach to Security." *Security Dialogue* 45 (1): 5-21.

Mol, Annemarie. 2002. *The Body Multiple: Ontology in Medical Practice*. Durham: Duke University Press.

Morton, Timothy. 2010. "Hyperobjects and The End of Common Sense." *The Contemporary Condition*, March 18. http://contemporarycondition.blogspot. de/2010/03/hyperobjects-and-end-of-common-sense.html

Morton, Timothy. 2013. *Hyperobjects: Philosophy and Ecology after the End of the World*. Minneapolis: University of Minnesota Press.

Moser, Ingunn. 2008. "Making Alzheimer's Disease Matter. Enacting, Interfering and Doing Politics of Nature." *Geoforum* 39 (1): 98-110.

Randalls, Samuel. 2015. "Creating Positive Friction in the Anthropo(s)cenes." *Dialogues in Human Geography* 5 (3): 333-336.

Schneider, Birgit, and Thomas Nocke, eds. 2014. *Image Politics of Climate Change: Visualizations, Imaginations, Documentations*. Bielefeld: Transcript.

Stavrakakis, Yannis. 1997. "Green Ideology: A Discursive Reading." *Journal of Political Ideologies* 2(3): 259-279.

Steffen, Will, Paul J. Crutzen, and John R. McNeill. 2007. "The Anthropocene: Are Humans Now Overwhelming The Great Forces of Nature." *AMBIO: A Journal of the Human Environment* 36 (8): 614-621.

Steffen, Will et al. 2015. "Planetary Boundaries: Guiding Human Development on a Changing Planet." *Science* 347 (6223): 1259855.

van Munster, Rens, and Casper Sylvest. 2016. "Introduction." In *The Politics of Globality Since 1945: Assembling the Planet*, edited by Rens van Munster, and Casper Sylvest, 1-19. New York: Routledge.

Vrasti, Wanda, and Nicholas Michelsen. 2016. "Introduction: On Resilience and Solidarity. Resilience." *International Policies, Practices and Discourses* 5 (1):1-9.

Wark, McKenzie. 2015a. "From OOO to P(OO)." Object Oriented Ontology Conference at The New School, New York, 2011. Public Seminar, 5 December 2015. http://www.publicseminar.org/2015/12/from-ooo-to-poo/#. WFvrwrGX-Rs (accessed 21 December 2016).

Wark, McKenzie. 2015b. *Molecular Red: Theory for the Anthropocene*. New York: Verso.

Yusoff, Kathryn. 2013. "The Geoengine: Geoengineering and The Geopolitics of Planetary Modification." *Environment and Planning A* 45 (12): 2799-2808.

Zalasiewicz, Jan, Mark Williams, Alan Haywood, and Michael Ellis. 2011. "The Anthropocene: A New Epoch of Geological Time? Philosophical Transactions of the Royal Society of London A." *Mathematical, Physical and Engineering Sciences* 369 (1938): 835-841.

Žižek, Slavoj. 2016. *Disparities*. London: Bloomsbury Publishing.

9

The 'Nature' of International Relations: From Geopolitics to the Anthropocene

OLAF CORRY

International Relations (IR) has been criticised for its exclusively human perspective and for having 'been little concerned with the vast variety of other, non-human populations of species and "things"' (Cudworth and Hobden 2013, 644). One aim of post-humanist work is to find a way of including the natural world in a meaningful way into IR theory and analysis (see Kaltofen this volume). This is a challenge, but perhaps not an insurmountable one. After all, the discipline has roots in geopolitical analysis of how geography and climates affect world politics. The brief 'natural history of IR' that follows is necessarily a broad-brush depiction of how IR has (not) theorised and analysed the natural world in various ways (Corry and Stevenson 2017b). It shows that IR, although similar to sociology that became 'radically sociological' (Buttel 1996, 57), is not immune to concern for the natural world, but also that there is a long track record of either reifying or ignoring it. The chapter concludes by considering how best to proceed in developing an IR as if the Earth matters.

Geopolitics and Nature

IR has some of its deepest disciplinary roots in considerations about geography. As Daniel Deudney pointed out, whereas 'recent literature typically casts nature as a new factor in politics, the idea that nature is a powerful force shaping human political institutions is extremely old' (1999 25-6). For Aristotle, climate and agricultural aspects of territory were behind the rise and spread of empires while Montesquieu argued that Asia and Europe had different political systems because of their geographies and modern writers have taken up similar *physiopolitical* themes (Diamond 1997; Crosby 2015[1986]). For Alexis de Tocqueville, nature itself was a factor in American democracy: 'it is not only legislation that is democratic; nature itself works for the people'; God had given them 'the means of remaining equal and free, by placing them upon a boundless continent' conveniently isolated from the anarchy of European inter-state relations (Tocqueville 2000, 267).

The 'geopolitics' tradition that emerged from around 150 years ago among European geographers, put the natural world at the centre of their analysis of world politics (see Haslam 2002, 162-182). This emerged in turn out of a shifting mix of geography, demographics, evolutionary ideas, racial theory and realist doctrine (Bashford 2014). In Britain, Halford J. Mackinder argued that geography, having charted the entire globe, then had to move on to analyse how humans live in and on the land and seas (1904). Best known for his Heartland Thesis – the idea that the central Eurasian landmass is the key to world domination – Mackinder saw land power as superior to sea power, reasoning that navies needed ports and docks to be built and operated from. In contrast, for Alfred Mahan, the sea presented itself 'as a great highway' that was until recently much easier to move on than land (Mahan 1890, 34). But for Mackinder the Heartland was impenetrable from the icy north and desert-covered south and mainly accessible to the west. This meant that the central drama of geopolitics was between Germans expanding East and Slavs in Eastern Europe who were in their way and competing for control of the 'pivot area'. Eurasia was effectively the 'pivot' of history.

Figure 1: Halford J. Mackinder's Heartland Theory map, as published in 1904

This cast nature as an anchor or determinant of international affairs. The Swedish geographer Rudolf Kjellén was the first to use the term 'geopolitics' in 1899, while German geographer Joseph Ratzel suggested he was conducting 'anthro-geographical' studies. With the term Lebensraum Ratzel aimed to describe how dynamic populations and states required space and resources, driving international conflict on a finite – and by that time fully charted – globe. Inspired by Darwinian and Malthusian thought, most infamously, geopolitics was appropriated instrumentally by the Nazis with the German geographer and general Karl Haushofer directly influencing Rudolf Hess with geopolitical ideas.

Geopolitics emphasised nature as a factor in world politics, but not as part of a vulnerable web of life. Rather, nature provided resources and a physical backdrop or stage upon which vigorous racial groups and nations engaged in struggles for power and resources. Thus nature, in pre-war geopolitics, is conceived of in firmly anthropocentric as well as state-centric terms as either a facilitator or hindrance to geopolitical expansion or defence of human groups.

Human nature

This changed with the advent of the modern post-WWII disciplinary IR. Geography as a determinant of politics fell into serious intellectual disrepute. Often labelled a 'classical realist', Hans Morgenthau in Politics Among Nations, declared geopolitics to be 'a pseudoscience erecting the factor of geography into an absolute that is supposed to determine the power, and hence the fate, of nations' (Morgenthau 1985, [1948], 174). Geography, Morgenthau admitted, could give 'one aspect of the reality of national power' but amounted to a 'distortion' (ibid.) on its own, especially when fused with virulent nationalism. Even today, geopolitics has to deflect suspicions and claim 'misappropriation' during the interwar years (Kaplan 2009, 61), some suggesting that the term geopolitik be used for the German interwar variant (Sicker 2010, 5).

In most accounts of classical realism, the main aspect of nature still taken seriously is human nature. In Morgenthau's 'Six Principles of Political Realism' the first is that 'politics is governed by objective laws that have their roots in human nature' (1985 [1948], 4). These laws had not changed 'since the classical philosophies of China, India and Greece' (ibid.) and finding and adhering to them meant accurately identifying human nature (rather than nature itself). On this account, the vast planes and mountain ranges of Asia were swapped for the mental schemata and drives of Homo Sapiens in general, and of statesmen (sic) in particular. Foreign policy should be guided by the concept of 'interest defined in the terms of power'. This depended, in turn, on 'the political and cultural context within which foreign policy is formulated' (ibid., 11).

Realism never relinquishes the issue of resources and territory, but they seem by now already to be subordinate to politics, interests and historical conjunctions that allowed these to take shape. Morgenthau is at pains not to reduce politics to anything else, including geography: 'Intellectually, the political realist maintains the autonomy of the political sphere, as the economist, the lawyer, the moralist maintain theirs' (ibid., 13). Critical of social science scientism, Morgenthau also objected to how 'geopolitics endeavoured to put foreign policy as a whole on a scientific basis' (1964, 94). Science itself was in any case not objective: even physicists viewed their 'own external world in a way which I can only describe as mystical', he commented (ibid., 134). Sounding like a modern constructivist Morgenthau argued that '(n)ature as the object of human knowledge is, therefore, somehow the product of human action' (Ibid., 141).

At the same time, post-war Realism was an incubator of, if not a strong sense of nature, then other expressions of materialism. Technology and economics were considered important mediators of power. In particular, Morgenthau, John Herz and others recognised that the nuclear revolution changed some foundational calculations of political order and conflict. Human appropriated forces of nature – technology – had become a significant condition for power politics. For some this also suggested a need to re-code some core realist ethics (van Munster and Sylvest 2016): going beyond concern for the national interest, 'global realist' thinking took as its point of departure the 'material existence of the globe as a single physical and sociopolitical space' (ibid, 10).

Nature and Modern IR Theory

However, by the time IR had moved beyond the first 'Great Debate' between realists and (imagined) idealists, to debates about scientific method and 'rigor', nature disappeared even further from view. If Morgenthau insisted on the irreducibility of politics, Kenneth Waltz and the neo-realists worked to establish the autonomy of the international from the rest of politics. Waltz' epistemological stance told him that 'in reality everything is connected to everything else' (Waltz 1979, 8), but also that scientific models should isolate an element of reality in order to render it amenable to analysis. A theory of international politics would therefore abstract from complexity (and hence history) and focus on regularities and structure.

With neorealism, the structure of international politics became a disembodied product of multiple competing units, irrespective of national cultures, geography or statesmen. Waltz had effectively airbrushed the physical backdrop to geopolitics away revealing an abstract neorealist formalism (Corry and Stevenson 2017a). Maps of the globe (see Figure 1) were replaced with schematic model representations (see figure 2).

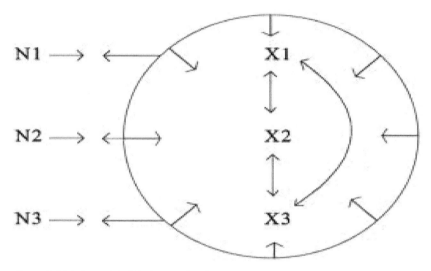

Figure 2: Waltz's model of the international system

'Capabilities' lingered as the strongest link in neo-realism back to a material sense of place and time: a state takes on the role of a pole in the system if it has relatively many capabilities including 'the size of population and territory, resource endowment, economic capacity, military strength, political stability and competence' (Waltz 1979, 131). But each state also became 'functionally equivalent', as each one had to solve essentially the same dilemmas. Hence, nature was ignored, or reduced to fungible resources of power. Notwithstanding occasional references to geography e.g. 'the stopping power of water' (Mearsheimer), for neorealists, 'place' became a function of economics, military strength and political affiliation.

Neoliberal Institutionalism, the main rival to neo-realism during the 1980s and 1990s, evolved out of functionalist and liberal traditions and was part of the effort to make IR into a social science. With its focus on rational actors, institutions, rules and incentives rather than place, history or drives, the physical and natural world became, if anything, even more consistently occluded from view. In Karl Deutsch's cybernetic approach, *communication* and 'systems of decisions, regulation and control' replaced 'drives' and 'instincts' as explanatory factors in international relations (Deutsch 1969

[1963], 77). Later, notions such as 'complex interdependence' (Keohane and Nye 1977) challenged realist nostrums but offered no alternative view of the natural world's place in international politics. 'Environment' and 'population' were cursorily included as examples of complex interdependence (Keohane and Nye 1977, 26) but most examples were drawn from the field of economics (Moravscik 2009, 245). Multinational firms, other non-state actors and inequalities worldwide were thought to be among the factors changing the basic codes of world politics undermining the distinctness of the units (states) and the high politics/low politics distinction that made up the basis of the realist states-in-anarchy model.

Liberalism has a strong human-centric impulse (although the transformative potential of technology has also been a theme in this tradition – see Deudney 2006, 193-214 for a summary of 'liberal historical materialism'). When 'neo-liberal institutionalism' emerged taking on board neo-realist notions of anarchy and state-centrism as well as a rational decision-maker model, the natural stage upon which rational state action and institution-building played out is perhaps implicitly assumed, but as such it is invisible. At least nature no longer figures in explanations or predictions of potential shifts or stability in world hegemony (Keohane 1984). Similarly, formal modelling in a rational-actor paradigm operates with disembodied 'social actors' and 'decision-makers', although, again, these may have access to 'resources'. The main determinant of actions is 'preferences' and 'information' (e.g. Keohane and Ostrom 1995).

Outside the two leading paradigms, Marxism of course had materialism as a founding tenet, and this remains the case in much contemporary IR theorists drawing on Marx – although a portion of Western Marxism with Lukács explicitly rejected a 'dialectics of nature' reserving dialectics to history and society (Foster 2013). In practice, post-Marxist IR-approaches have focused on economic structures, dependency in terms of social and economic development and overarching 'world systems' (Wallerstein 1974). Alternatively, hegemonic projects anchored in (currently neoliberal) forms of social organization and ideology (Cox 1981) have taken analytical precedence over analysis of human interaction with nature directly (Mészáros 1970).

Uneven and Combined Development theory has recently been developed and has touched at times on the role of natural features of regions and countries in establishing and perpetuating unevenness (Rosenberg 2013) – or on these and the role of non-human (but highly social) factors such as pandemics (Anievas and Nisancioglu 2015, 81-82). Neither nature nor human nature here are considered a-historical quantities, yet neither is subsumed under 'national interests' or abstracted away via rational decisionism. Historical materialist method thus has perhaps the most immediate potential in terms of providing theoretical apparatus for including nature in IR and allowing for analysis of dialectical relations between nature and human societies (see below).

Constructivist and post-structuralist approaches arrived just as Marxist perspectives faltered towards and after the end of the Cold War. Reflectivist approaches were opposed to rationalism, but did little to change the marginalization of 'nature' in IR. Alexander Wendt advanced a predominantly idealist and social constructivist view of international relations, though he reserved a space for 'rump materialism' (Wendt 1999, 110). The latter included 'human nature, a weak version of technological determinism and geography/natural resources' (Guzzini and Leander 2006, 78) although this, Wendt admitted, was relatively inconsequential for his theoretical setup (Wendt 1999, 136). Post-structuralism with its focus on discourses and structures of signification ventured further down the anti-materialist route, eradicating the 'rump' of materialism, albeit in terms of epistemology more than ontology. Commonly post-structuralists do not deny the existence of 'the external world' – external to discourse – but materiality takes on a shadowy existence as an essentially unknowable entity that is accessible and effective only through signification and social institutions which are typically imbued with language and meaning rather than matter.

Nature as 'Environment'

Instead, nature reappears in IR from around the 1970s, not as a constitutive factor underpinning world politics but in the guise of 'the environment' – as an issue or problem to be managed (Corry and Stevenson 2017a). This partly reflects the way it appeared. While military-related technologies such as satellites, space-travel and climate models prepared the way, environmental issues such as climate change were pushed by scientists, international organizations and popular environmental movements worried about environmental limits (Edwards 2010).

This inserted a different, but still firmly anthropocentric, view of nature into IR with a 'separation of the 'human' from other species, natures and entities' (Cudworth and Hobden 2013, 643). While it stimulated analysis and theorising, it did not initially bring the natural world into the IR theories themselves. The collective action-framing of environmental problems was a major impetus to the formulation of regime theory, but this focused on principles, rules, norms and procedures (e.g. Krasner 1982; Young 1989). 'Regime complexes' – overlapping institutions and norms that are formally distinct but functionally linked – were similarly prompted by analysis of the patchwork of climate change institutions and norms (Raustiala and Victor 2004; Keohane and Victor 2011). Environmental issues also provided a major occasion for the 'epistemic communities' literature to enter International Relations (Adler and Haas, 1992) and new global challenges such as ozone depletion and other cases that suggested a prominent role for scientific knowledge in international politics have more recently inspired more interaction with Science and Technology Studies (STS) (Beck and Forsyth 2017).

Meanwhile 'the environment' also became a feature of realist lineage. This can be seen notably in debates about environmental security (Homer-Dixon 1994; Dalby 2002) and resource scarcity and conflict (see Jan Selby 2014 for a critique). More recently this debate has been framed in terms of 'climate security' (see McDonald 2013 for an overview). Securitization Theory was developed partly to accommodate environmental 'referent objects' of security (Wæver 1995) and recent expansions of the Copenhagen School of security studies seek to encompass 'macro-securitizations' that arise from global risks such as climate change (Buzan and Wæver 2009). Recently English School writers have begun considering whether environmental stewardship is gradually becoming a 'primary institution' of international society and sovereignty (Falkner 2017).

The New Geopolitics and the Anthropocene

At the same time, the geopolitics of old is having something of a renaissance. Reconnecting directly to the pre-war geopolitics, writers such as Robert Kaplan announced the 'revenge of geography' (2009) and Patrick Porter has sought to dispel the 'myth of the global village' (2015). For both – and other post-classical realists (see Brooks 1997), the overall argument is that world politics is still underpinned by geography that conditions the ease or difficulty projecting power, even given the technological innovations such as the Internet and aviation. Globalization and technological changes modulate the significance of geography, but they do not negate it. Mackinder and the others were 'misused' by the Nazis, they say (Kaplan 2013, 61), to fashion a crude determinism, and the baby was thrown out with the bathwater.

More problematically, related ideas are currently espoused by Alexandr Dugin, a neofascist Russian sociologist who has advised amongst others the speaker of the Russian Duma. Dugin claims also to draw on the work of Mackinder, Kjellén and other geopolitical thinkers but espouses the view that the strategic aim for Russia should be to head a Eurasian empire, carve up Central Asia and Europe with an expanded Germany, while destabilising and undermining the Atlanticist US-led world order. Allegedly influential in Moscow, Dugin recommends using all means available including (cyber-) subversion and war against the West (Dunlop 2004; d'Ancona 2016).

But while reintroducing geography, this literature neither engages the 'environmental' question, nor the planetary ethics of the 'nuclear realists', casting some doubt also on the transformative power of technologies. Mackinder, Ratzel and Kjellén focused on the implications of geophysical structures for world politics - not the other way around. Humans are connected to it in so far as it provides resources or erects barriers to power. Others outside IR, notably critical geographers have long viewed geography as something mediated by social institutions, histories and discourses (O' Tuathail and Agnew 1992). Simon Dalby has suggested that what is needed is an Anthropocence geopolitics. The politics of knowing and governing geophysical systems of the planet is a different problem to the classical one of navigating power politics: '(g)eopolitics is no longer just about playing the great game of state rivalry; it is also now literally about remaking the playing field' as the ice caps melt and the climate heads for a new, hotter equilibrium state: 'the current geopolitics is determining the future climate of the planet. Political and business leaders are effectively deciding whether there will be polar ice caps on the planet a couple of centuries from now' (2014, 3). Similarly, Earth Systems Governance literature explores how dynamic and vulnerable natural systems and 'planetary boundaries' can be negotiated (Biermann 2014; Rockström et al. 2009). STS has made an impact on IR too (Acuto and Curtis 2014; Beck and Forsyth 2017), though its wariness of grand theory puts a limit on this.

This covers some international issues, but more fundamentally, how should canonical categories in IR such as sovereignty, anarchy and balance of power be re-thought in an Anthropocene age (Corry 2016)?

Nature/Human: Synthesis or Dialectics?

There are of course numerous ways to go about answering such a puzzle. To simplify, some proceed by blurring the distinction between the human and the non-human (Kaltofen, this volume) or between social and natural. For instance, Audra Mitchell has suggested the term 'worldly security' encompassing the physical, built environment and cultures of human communities (2014) and she draws on Isabelle Stenger's notion of 'cosmopolitics' according to which 'human and nonhuman, living and non-living, organic and inorganic — can intervene in politics by 'forcing thought' through their effects, properties, presence or absence' (Mitchell 2016, 17). Some STS approaches including Actor-Network Theory would tend to point in a similar direction using the concepts of 'actant' and 'assemblage' to indicate a hybrid ontology of natural and social systems (Latour 1990; see also Acuto and Curtis 2014).

Other critical posthuman approaches do, however, emphasise the continuing importance of boundaries between humans and nonhumans, but aim to specify the 'embeddedness' of humans in the non-human: 'We need to take analytic account of both differences and distinctions as well as the ways in which beings and things (including ourselves, of course) are co-constituted' (Cudworth and Hobden 2013, 644).

Breaking down the analytical distinction between human and non-human, the challenge is to not subsume one under the other: either risk treating all natural systems as pliable and socially constructed; or treating social life as simply a subset of the natural world, rendered from the same matter and subject to the same (scientific) methods of knowing. With James Lovelock's (once-controversial, now less so) Gaia-theory, the Earth is considered one single self-regulating organism, and humans can potentially be dispensed with as a result of Anthropocene changes, or could possibly survive and act as Gaia's 'brain' (Lovelock 2009, 248). Just as anthropocentrism renders the natural world incidental to analysis, Lovelock's eco-centrism recognises that human society is dispensable to the Earth (Lovelock 2006).

The other strategy is to maintain that humans and society on the one hand, and natural systems on the other, deserve their own terminologies and theories. Although they are increasingly linked – and in the Anthropocene inextricably so – they represent different analytical logics and are best theorised as such. Here the major challenge is then to specify in a satisfactory manner *how* they relate to each other. This can be as distinct but interlinked entities or spheres, or perhaps in terms of *dialectics* between humans and nature: one conditions and transforms the other, which in turn acts back upon the first in its new form, recreating the point of departure for the next historical and iterative development.

While new materialism is promising, an 'old materialism' emphasising the dialectics of nature and history should also be explored more fully. Marx put nature, and human interaction with it, right at the centre of a historical social theory (Foster 2000). Production and technology mediated between humans and nature, with the latter two conditioning the other as well as technology: 'For Marx, human beings transformed their relation to nature but not exactly as they pleased; they did so in accordance with conditions inherited from the past and as a result of a complex process of historical development that reflected a changing relation to a natural world, which was itself dynamic in character' (Foster 1999, 390). Uneven and Combined Development theory inserts a specifically international dimension into these dialectics (Rosenberg 2013).

But dialectical method is not confined to Marxism. The transformation of the natural world that the 'Anthropocene' captures, and the transformation of the human that 'post-humanism' aims for, could be considered two sides of an accelerating dialectic. This requires some explications that are beyond this essay. But even in more prosaic terms, there is a dialectical interchange implied in some existing interpretations of environment and security. In Ole Wæver's seminal essay *securitization/desecuritization* the environment is just one of several possible 'valued referent objects' of security, i.e. which is threatened and requiring exceptional means to defend it (1995). This keeps the environment ontologically separate yet implicated in the political logic of 'security'. That logic itself in turn grew out of specific historical conditions after the end of WWII (Wæver 1995). In dialectical terms the story does not stop there, either. Articulations of environmental security might be transforming the logic of security anew (Trombetta 2008). In this volume, Matt McDonald considers the idea of 'ecological security' (2016) as a way of moving beyond anthropocentric notions of environmental security. This clearly involves more than applying a familiar notion of security to the biosphere, requiring instead a new idea of security. Which again provides the basis for a new understanding of 'environment', and so forth.

Although IR is a thoroughly anthropocentric discipline, nature has featured prominently, albeit quite differently and sporadically. From the *physiopolitics* of the Greeks, via European *geopolitics* to the more recent *global environmental politics*, this legacy bears remembering while we search for a stronger sense of materiality and a framework for accounting for the natural world in IR theory. The post-war rationalist and constructivist paradigms perhaps marginalised nature most starkly. Classical realists engage with territory and technology but with the ascent of a social scientific epistemology, geopolitics and historical materialism marginalised. The concept of 'the environment' involved a pigeonholing of nature, which became, at best, a human collective action problem.

The challenge now is to find a way forward that does not simply revive geography as a condition of great power competition, but rather one that grapples with an *Anthropocene IR*: how do we rethink IR for a world where humanity, the international system and the Earth's current ecology are mutually transformative – and potentially mutually destructive? If the main thrust of post-humanism and political ecology has been to deconstruct the distinction between human and non-human, alternative modes – such as viewing the relationship as a dialectical one – deserve more systematic attention. Although, in the end, both will doubtless be necessary if there is to be a discipline of IR as if the Earth mattered (Corry and Stevenson 2017b).

References

Acuto, Michele, and Simon Curtis. 2014. *Reassembling International Theory.* Basingstoke: Palgrave Macmillan.

Adler, Emanuel, and Peter M. Haas. 1992. "Conclusion: Epistemic Communities, World Order, and The Creation of a Research Program." *International Organization* 46 (1): 367-390.

Anievas, Alex, and Kerem Nisancioglu. 2015. *How the West Came to Rule.* Chicago: University of Chicago Press Economics Books.

Bashford, Alison. 2014. *Global Population: History, Geopolitics and Life on Earth.* Columbia University Press.

Beck, Silke, and Tim Forsyth. 2017. "Environmental Science and International Relations." In *Traditions and Trends in Global Environmental Politics. International Relations and the Earth,* edited by Olaf Corry and Hayley Stevenson. UK: Routledge.

Brooks, Stephen G., 1997. "Dueling Realisms." *International Organization* 51 (3):445-477.

Buttel, Frederick H., 1996. "Environmental and Resource Sociology: Theoretical Issues and Opportunities for Synthesis." *Rural Sociology* 61 (1): 56–76.

Buzan, Barry, and Ole Wæver. 2009. "Macrosecuritisation and Security Constellations: Reconsidering Scale in Securitisation Theory." *Review of International Studies* 35 (2): 253-276.

Cudworth, Erika, and Stephen Hobden. 2013. "Complexity, Ecologism and Post-Human Politics." *Review of International Studies* 39 (3): 643–664.

Corry, Olaf. 2016. "Saving IR from the Anthropocene: Societal multiplicity, Governance-Objects and Climate Change." Paper presented at EWIS, Tübingen April 5th, 2016.

Corry Olaf, and Hayley. Stevenson. 2017a. "Societal Multiplicity and Planetary Singularity. International Relations and the Earth." In *Traditions and Trends in Global Environmental Politics. International Relations and the Earth,* edited by Olaf Corry and Hayley Stevenson. UK: Routledge.

Corry Olaf, and Hayley Stevenson. 2017b. "International Relations as if the Earth Mattered." In *Traditions and Trends in Global Environmental Politics. International Relations and the Earth.* UK: Routledge.

Cox, Robert W., 1981. "Social Forces, States and World Orders: Beyond International Relations Theory." *Millennium* 10 (2):126-155.

Crosby, Alfred W., 2015. *Ecological Imperialism: The Biological Expansion of Europe 900-1900* (second ed.) Cambridge: Cambridge University Press.

Dalby, Simon. 2002. *Environmental Security*. London: University of Minnesota Press.

Dalby, Simon. 2014. "Environmental Geopolitics in the Twenty-First Century." *Alternatives: Global, Local, Political* 39 (1): 3-16.

D'Ancona, Matthew. 2016. "Putin and Trump Could be on The Same Side in this Troubling New World Order.", *The Guardian,* December *19.* Accessible online. https://www.theguardian.com/world/commentisfree/2016/dec/19/trump-putin-same-side-new-world-order

Deudney, Daniel. 1999. "Bringing Nature Back in: Geopolitical Theory from the Greeks to the Global Era." In *Contested grounds: Security and Conflict in the New Environmental Politics,* edited by Daniel Deudney, and Richard A. Matthew, 25-57. New York: Albany State University Press.

Deudney, Daniel. 2006. *Bounding Power: Republican Security Theory from the Polis to the Global Village.* Princeton: Princeton University Press.

Deutsch, Karl. 1969. *The Nerves of Government: Models of Political Communication and Control.* New York: The Free Press, 3rd ed.

Diamond, Jared. 1997. *Guns, Germs and Steel: The Fates of Human Societies.* New York: W.W. Norton.

Dunlop, John B., 2004. "Aleksandr Dugin's Foundations of Geopolitics." *Demokratizatsiya* 12 (1):41.

Edwards, Paul N., 2010. *A Vast Machine: Computer Models, Climate Data, and the Politics of Global Warming.* Massachusetts: MIT Press.

Falkner, Robert. 2017 "International Climate Politics Between Pluralism and Solidarism: An English School perspective." In *Traditions and Trends in Global Environmental Politics. International Relations and the Earth,* edited by Olaf Corry and Hayley Stevenson UK: Routledge.

Foster, John B., 1999. "Marx's Theory of Metabolic Rift: Classical Foundations for Environmental Sociology." *American Journal of Sociology* 105 (2): 366-405.

Foster, John B., 2013. "Marx and the Rift in the Universal Metabolism of Nature". *Monthly Review* 65 (7):1-19.

Guzzini, Stefano, and Anna Leander, eds. 2006. *Constructivism and International Relations: Alexander Wendt and his Critics.* London: Routledge.

Haslam, Jonathan. 2002. *No Virtue like Necessity. Realist Thought in International Relations since Machiavelli.* London: Yale University Press.

Homer-Dixon, Thomas F., 1994. "Environmental Scarcities and Violent Conflict: Evidence from Cases". *International Security* 19 (1):5-40.

Kaltofen, Carolin. 2017. "The spectrum of human critical humanism(s)." in Eroukhmanoff, C. and M. Harker (eds) (2017) *The Posthuman,* E-International Relations.

Kaplan, Robert. 2009. 'The Revenge of Geography." *Foreign Policy* 172: 96-105.

Kaplan, Robert. 2013. *The Revenge of Geography. What the Map Tells us about Coming Conflicts and the Battle Against Fate.* New York: Random House.

Keohane, Robert. 1984, *After Hegemony. Cooperation and Discord in the World Political Economy.* New Jersey: Princeton University Press.

Keohand, Robert, and Elinor Ostrom, eds. 1995. *Local Commons and Global Interdependence.* London: Sage.

Keohane, Robert O., and Joseph S. Nye. 1977. *Power and interdependence: World politics in transition* (2nd ed). Boston: Little, Brown.

Keohane, Robert O., and David G. Victor. 2011. "The Regime Complex for Climate Change." *Perspectives on Politics* 9 (1): 7-23.

Krasner, Stephen D., 1982. "Structural Causes and Regime Consequences: Regimes as Intervening Variables." *International Organization* 36 (2): 185-205.

Latour, Bruno. 1990. "Technology is Society Made Durable." *The Sociological Review* 38 (1):103-131.

Lovelock James. 2006. *Revenge of Gaia: Why the Earth is Fighting Back and How We Can Still Save Humanity.* London: Allen Lane.

Lovelock, James. 2009. *The Vanishing Face of Gaia: A Final Warning.* London: Allen Lane.

McDonald, Matt. 2013. "Discourses of Climate Security." *Political Geography* 33: 42-51.

Mackinder, Halford J., 1904. "The Geographical Pivot of History." *The Geographical Journal* 23 (4):421-437.

Mahan, Alfred T., 1890. *The Influence of Sea Power upon History, 1660-1783.* Boston: Little, Brown and Co.

Mészáros, Istvan. 1970. *Marx's Theory of Alienation.* London: Merlin Press.

Moravcsik, Andrew. 2009. "Robert Keohane: Political Theorist." In *Power, Interdependence and Non-State Actors in World Politics: Research Frontiers,* edited by Helen V Milner, and Andrew Moravscik, 243-263. Oxford: Princeton University Press.

Morgenthau, Hans J., 1985. *Politics Among Nations,* revised by Kenneth W. Thompson. New York: Knopf.

Morgenthau, Hans J., 1946. *Scientific Man versus Power Politics.* London: University of Chicago Press.

Mitchell, Audra. 2014. "Only Human? A Worldly Approach to Security." *Security Dialogue* 45(1):5-21.

Porter, Patrick. 2015. *The Global Village Myth: Distance, War, and the Limits of Power.* Washington: Georgetown University Press.

Raustiala, Kal, and David G. Victor. 2004. "The Regime Complex for Plant Genetic Resources." *International Organization* 58 (2): 277–309.

Rockström, Johan, et al. Foley 2009. "A Safe Operating Space for Humanity." *Nature* 461(7263): 472-475.

Rosenberg, Justin. 2013. "The 'Philosophical Premises' of Uneven and Combined Development." *Review of International Studies* 39 (3): 569-597.

Selby, Jan. 2014. "Positivist Climate Conflict Research: A Critique." *Geopolitics* 19 (4): 829-856.

Sicker, Martin. 2010. *Geography and Politics Among Nations: An Introduction to Geopolitics.* New York: iUniverse Inc.

Tocqueville, Alexis. de. 2000. *Democracy in America.* ed. Harvey C. Mansfield, trans. Harvey C. Mansfield, Delba Winthrop. Chicago: University of Chicago Press.

Trombetta, Maria Julia. 2008. "Environmental Security and Climate Change: Analysing the Discourse." *Cambridge Review of International Affairs* 21 (4): 585- 602.

Tuathail, Gearóid Ó., and John Agnew. 1992. "Geopolitics and Discourse: Practical Geopolitical Reasoning in American Foreign Policy." *Political Geography* 11 (2): 190-204.

Young, Oran. 1989. *International Cooperation: Building Regimes for Natural Resources and the Environment.* Ithaca: Cornell University Press

Van Munster, Rens, and Casper Sylvest. 2016. *Nuclear Realism: Global Political Thought during the Thermonuclear Revolution.* London: Routledge.

Wallerstein, Immanuel. 1974. *The Modern World-System: Capitalist Agriculture and the Origins of the European World-Economy in the Sixteenth Century.* New York: Academic Press.

Waltz, Kenneth. 1979. *Theory of International Politics.* New York: McGraw Hill

Wendt, Alexander. 1999. *A Social Theory of International Politics.* Cambridge: Cambridge University Press.

Wæver, Ole. 1995. "Securitization/De-securitization." In *On Security,* edited by Ronnie D. Lipschutz New York: Columbia University Press.

10

Metternich, The Gut-Brain Axis, and the Turing Cops: The Subjects of Posthuman IR

DARIAN MEACHAM

Is a Posthuman World a World without Human-subjectivity?

Approaching the relation between posthumanism and international relations (IR) from some disciplinary distance, there seem, at first pass, fewer more awkward intellectual travelling companions. The very idea of a nation is to a large extent tied up historically and epistemologically with the idea of the human being, and more precisely the human subject of the human sciences. More specifically, nations are social institutions that are constituted by conscious, active, and supposedly autonomous human subjects who identify with the nation in a reciprocal process of institutional reinforcement creating in the process both the nation and national-subjects. Whether one adheres to a primordialist positon that modern nation-states are founded upon proto-national communities or a modernist one that the socio-economic conditions of the industrial age created a need for a new political form, the nation-state, and a new political subject, the national citizen, it is the case that modern nations are institutions that require speaking, remembering, interacting subjects, in other words, subjects that navigate the world like us. That's not to say that other forms of political life are not possible for human-subjects, they obviously are, but rather that there seems to be a special relation and perhaps one of dependency between nations and certain types of subjects. And in gratitude for their existence the nation-state provides these newly instituted subjects a pole around which to situate an identity and orient relations with other (human) subjects, as well promising a degree of material security and stability to accompany the spiritual.

The nationalities of non-human subjects are, pet passports notwithstanding, irrelevant to the perseverance of the nation. If in a radical form the project of post-humanism proposes radically altering the human-subject, this will likely mean altering the viability or even possibility of the nation-state as a political form. This may of course be a desirable outcome, but then our questions about posthuman security will no longer involve nations and their subjects as the central actors of this drama and so a posthuman post-IR will have to undertake rethinking both sides of this dyad. Harrington (this volume) notes that 'To speak of security absent the human subject has been considered irrational or worse, uninteresting.' I might provocatively go one step further, speech, absent the human subject, does not seem to me to be something that we can speak about (cf. David Roden 2015 on speculative post-humanism and the 'disconnection thesis').

Moreover, concrete and historical international relations have to some extent developed in the modern period alongside the sciences of and variations on the theme of the subject. Metternich's Concert of Europe was designed to suppress or at least control the growing power of national subjectivity: the idea being that truly great, autonomous, sovereign men would meet one another in order to settle disputes and retain not only their balance of territorial power, but also their power over and against the mass of newly formed national subjects whose national desires and ambitions, though in some cases stoked by these same great men for various purposes, threatened to grow out of control, overturning established orders.[22] Metternich's geo-political dream of an orderly European theatre of interstate relations came unravelled, at least in part, precisely due to the growing power of the mass political mobilization and mass parties which began to exert influence on domestic and international relations. This new form of suddenly politically relevant and active human being, the mass subject, was technologically mediated in its appearance through the proliferation of communication technologies and growing literacy among the labouring classes, which made representation by mass parties, with their correlative mechanisms of internal and external governance, possible.

The rise in influence of mass parties in (European) international relations is correlated to the emergence of a new form of political subjectivity and power, the mass-subject of disciplinary power that Michel Foucault investigates in such works as *The Birth of the Clinic* (1963) and *Discipline and Punish: the birth of the prison* (1975). The development of the human, social, and life

---

[22]   The so-called congress system of European international relations did also have a basis in law. The final act of the Vienna Congress stipulated that the border arrangements established by the congress could not be altered without agreement from the eight signatories (Soutou 2000).

sciences in whose frame the human subject gained its sense as an at least potentially rational and autonomous agent facilitated the growth of the techniques would be used to undermine this rational autonomy in the creation of the plastic, normalizable and administered subject of mass-society. This is not the place of course to recount this full story and the point of this grossly incomplete sketch of the development of the relation between the institution of the human subject and the institution of the nation-state is merely to point out a correlation between the development of the modern subject and the modes and actors of international relations. As Harrington (this volume) notes, 'exploration of alternative political identities beyond the state – such as nations, races, classes, movements, religions, cultures, or gender' (Walker 1993, cited by Harrington) are not foreign to IR and I do not wish to present an overtly state-centric idea of contemporary IR. But I think that the point holds, as the universe of IR expands to include institutions other than states, such as those mentioned above, the centrality of the human subject remains.

What Foucault, among others, shows is that the human-subject is not a fixed-essence with determinate capacities and structures of engaging with the world and others in it. Rather, sciences and technologies of the subject have developed in correlation with the sciences, techniques, and institutions of political life. Further developments, such as the discovery (if that is the right term) of the Anthropocene, discussed at considerable length throughout this volume, necessitate again a rethinking of this relation between the institutions of human-subjectivity and the *polis*.

The question then is what shift in our thinking about political institutions and specifically international relations and security will be enacted if we try to take seriously the idea of the post-human as a possible next chapter in this story of the modern (European?) human subject. A presupposition and a possible paradox should be noted here. First, I presuppose that the notion of the post-human has not only to do with the human as a biological entity, an individual of a group defined by one or another species concept,[23] but also, and perhaps primarily, with a specific type of subjectivity, namely the conscious, rational, and autonomous agent described by modern philosophy, and perhaps most exemplary, the addressee of the opening of Immanuel Kant's essay 'What Is Enlightenment' who has only to free himself of his 'self-imposed immaturity' (Kant 1784). Schwarz (this volume) makes a similar point, arguing that security, ethics and politics are fundamentally human constructs. I wish to push this point a bit further, emphasising aspects of specifically human subjectivity.   Thus, the significance of the 'posthuman' in the idea of posthuman international relations and security pertains not only to a

---

[23]   See here for a short list of species concepts. http://science.kennesaw.
edu/~rmatson/Biol%203380/3380species.html

questioning, critique, or de-centering of humans qua individuals or population of a particular species, but also to the status of a certain form of subjectivity or relation between the individuals of this particular biological species, other members of that species, and the surrounding milieu, including of course the individuals and populations of the rapidly dwindling multitude of other species that make up perhaps the most significant part of our human (species) milieu. The possible paradox stems from the presupposition.

The point that I hoped to make in the paragraphs above is that the political form of the nation is closely tied, perhaps inextricably, to a certain understanding of the human subject. It is not just that there are no nations and no politics without subjects, but also no speech without subjects. If the posthuman entails the end or transformation of the specific type of subjectivity proper to the political form of the nation, it makes sense to ask how viable the very notion of posthuman politics or inter-*national* relations may be, and what security premium we might be willing to pay to maintain the form of subjectivity proper and necessary to the nation. Thus I am in obvious agreement with Mitchell (this volume) when she argues that it is 'not possible to entirely escape the constructs, norms and shared experiences that help to define one's life as human' and also Rothe (this volume) in having a suspicion about any normative claim to overcome the subject/object divide. However, I do not think that we can have anything meaningful to say about what it is like to experience, know or act beyond the constraints of subjective life, let alone conceive of a politics beyond the subject/object divide.

Politics is classically and I think ultimately about the life of the *polis*, a life in common shared by human, subjective individuals. If we abandon, either epistemologically or ontologically the preconditions of this form of life, i.e. subjectivity, I think that we are stepping into a political unknown. I am less than convinced that, given the challenges introduced largely by the havoc modern human subjects (and perhaps one should add here, European) and their political forms have visited upon this planet, those we now associate with the term Anthropocene, we should be too quick to jettison either in our thinking or our doing, the precondition and indeed constraints of modern political life before asking what institutions can follow. I should be clear that I consider the human subject one of the foundational institutions of modern political life; it is an institution that while foundational of other political institutions, is also continuously acted upon and transformed by them. The point then, as Fishel (this volume) argues, is not to abandon but to recast the institution of the subject such that it is capable of fostering more 'just and peaceful relationships' with other subjects and with other entities in its milieu. Youatt (this volume) makes a similar claim in arguing that thinking how the notion of the posthuman could enter into IR discourse entails staying 'with the production of different kinds of humans as a question of political analysis.'

Thus it is certain that insofar as a posthuman world would mean a post-subjective world, it will be a world without us as we know us or could think about knowing us. As this volume demonstrates, this is by far not the only meaning of the posthuman, but it is I think an important one to grapple with. From an ecological perspective that tries to place the value of human-subjective life within a broader value context, wherein other forms of life (non-human animals, plants, bacteria, etc.) may have value claims made on their behalf which equal or even outweigh human claims, a world without human subjects is indeed likely to be a more secure or flourishing world. The South African philosopher David Benatar (2006) has recently made an argument against the continued proliferation of the human species. His argument revolves around the inevitability of human suffering; but our own species' self-concern aside, it seems a safe bet that the nonhuman subjects of this planet would be grateful for such a decision, and those parts of the biome not capable of such subject-object relations as gratitude better off.

The defence of the human subject that I have tabled here certainly does not mean that we cannot be critical of the notion of the subject. It is indubitably not the case that we must retain a vision of IR or global-security like the one imagined by Hans Morgenthau (see Corry, this volume), wherein a science of immutable human nature was necessary to understand and order global politics. The development of evolutionary biology has already rendered such an idea of human nature untenable. As Hull (1986, p.11) argues, 'any attempt to base anything, including ethics or politics, on human nature is basing it on historical happenstance.'

Thinking Ecologically about Ourselves or Centrifugal-anthropocentrism

An approach to posthuman IR and security that I would call ecological thinking or centrifugal-anthropocentrism, starts from the notion of posthumanism as a decentring critique of the primacy of certain forms or conceptions of human-subjectivity and argues for an ecological repositioning of the human. The term ecological here can be understood in two ways. On the one hand is the clear emphasis on ecologies as the focus of IR and security discourses. Ecologies can of course be seen as problems to be managed toward various human ends, this is the position of climate-change-updated traditional forms of IR and security discourse. The more radical way of thinking the relation between ecologies and security, as suggested by McDonald (this volume) is to orient security discourse 'towards the resilience of ecosystems themselves, with this in turn enabling the protection of the most vulnerable across time, space and species.' There seems to me to be a risk here that this orientation may reveal to us that the presence of our species has, generally speaking, a negative impact on the ecosystems that now become our primary security concern. But an ecological systems approach to security, even while retaining a weak anthropocentric presupposition, i.e. acknowledging the 'embeddedness of humans in complex worlds co-constituted by diverse beings' (Mitchell 2014 and this volume) – still seems a positive step forward toward greater planetary and indeed human security even if it retains an admittedly more relational and inter-dependent notion of human life as its central concern.

The idea of ecology is also relevant in another manner already suggested by weak anthropocentrism. The human subject can itself be considered from an ecological perspective, not just as functioning within ecologies, but as constituted within them. Gut flora is a clear example of this; human microbiota are essential to many basic vital human functions, and disturbances within the gut microbiome can be extremely detrimental to human health. The same holds for other species. It is not just digestive function that can be characterised ecologically, the 'gut microbiota is associated with metabolic disorders such as obesity, diabetes mellitus and neuropsychiatric disorders such as schizophrenia, autistic disorders, anxiety disorders and major depressive disorders' (Evrensel and Ceylan 2015, p.239). In other words, fundamental dimensions of what are considered normal and abnormal human subjective functions are linked not to a central pole of consciousness or the like but ecological systems constituted in part of other organisms in which human subjectivity is constituted and without which it is not possible. What such studies call into question is precisely the otherness of other organisms and the unity or sameness of ourselves; an ecological approach to subjectivity demonstrates that the subject does not belong to a unitary species or a unitary body, if that body is somehow purified of its constitutive relations with its surrounding milieu. The so-called 'gut-brain axis' points, in a very concrete fashion, to a way of thinking about posthumanism from a radical and perhaps Deleuzian perspective. As Kaltofen (this volume) puts it this 'radical end' of the posthuman spectrum contends that 'bodies are not bound by skin, but rather by flows of affect and intensity; where thought is not human in origin, but non-local and presubjective.' I am not sure if the gut-brain axis illustrates all of this, but it does certainly offer a case for saying that thought can be partially inhuman in its constitution; or perhaps better that the human-subject as normally described in its cognitive, rational and affective capacities is ecological in its formation, and that the ecology of the human subject contains a multitude of different species.

Insofar as we are still concerned with the condition and perhaps the flourishing of the human subject, that is, insofar as we remain at least 'weakly anthropocentric', our anthropocentrism has to become centrifugal (and in the case of gut flora centripetal). This means not only broadening the universe of IR to not just include but place at its centre, ecological well-being. At the same time, while I maintain that the notion of IR does not make sense outside of the frame of subjectivity, ecological thinking forces us to consider the constitution of the subject qua ecology as relational, integrated, impure. One outcome from this might be to say that the human subject is one of the ecologies that we should aim to secure so that it maintains certain capacities that we consider necessary for flourishing; and capacities that allow it to minimise the risk it poses to other ecologies *and to its own*. An ecology of the human-subject is constituted in part by some cell populations that we call our own, gut microbes, technologies like writing, political institutions like human rights, etc. I think that what is important here is understanding how to maintain an equilibrium in which capacities that we value emerge and persist.

So what is called for is an approach that views the concerns of IR or security discourse within nested ecologies which contain, gut-microbiota, organs, human and nonhuman subjects, etc. as well as institutions such as the nation-state or international governance bodies? Security, in this context means maintaining certain ecologies, including the ecology of the human-subject and taking seriously the idea of inter-dependence and co-constitution that sits at the heart of ecological thinking. Jon Turney (2016) has recently discussed the use of militarised immunity language in medical discourse. We can flip this and critique the use of militarised immune metaphors in security discourse. Attempts to isolate nested ecologies from their milieu as though they were self-sufficient substances and not networks of interchange, and this includes attempts to isolate the subject either epistemically or environmentally, only make them more fragile. Turney argues that it is time to abandon outdated notions of how the immune systems works which conceive of it as a barrier against threats to bodily integrity. Instead as the gut-microbiota example illustrates, '[t]he immune system keeps host and microbiome in equilibrium. There is continual action and reaction, like the give and take of a regular conversation. The results help to nurture some bacteria, while reducing opportunities for others (Turney 2016). This revised immune thinking should take its place not only in relation to how we conceive the body, but also how we think about the broader posthuman ecology of IR and security discourse. We need to maintain equilibriums in ecologies that we value. One such ecology may be the human subject itself.

Call the Turing Cops?

In William Gibson's famous cyberpunk novel Neuromancer (1984), the Turing Police are an international law enforcement agency who monitor and enforce laws pertaining to the behavior of artificial intelligences. It is curious that in a volume devoted to posthuman IR and security the subject of big data and associated phenomena (cf. Boyd and Crawford 2011) seem not to be at the forefront. There is no call to start training Turing Cops in this volume. Nonetheless, it is certainly the case that many if not all of the contributions here acknowledge that human-machine hybridity – or the technological mediation of the human being – is a central concern for post-human thinking. The anthropologist Leroi-Gourhan (1973) characterises the emergence of the human precisely by the 'exteriorization' of capacities through technology. I do not think that arguments in favour of epistemological, ontological or normative human-machine hybridity depart from the domain of human subjectivity conceived ecologically. To the contrary, one can argue, as Leroi-Gourhan does, that subjectivity only emerges in this technological hybridity or exteriorisation.

Yet, it seems a pressing question for posthuman IR and security to ask what challenges or threats are posed by the advent of big data technologies and how the insertion of these technologies into natural-institutional ecologies like the ones mentioned briefly above is likely to alter their configurations and the capacities that they produce. Danaher (2016) refers to the threat of 'algocracy': algorithms are increasingly being assigned control over political decision making-processes. Danaher concludes that we are increasingly divesting governance processes of possibilities for human participation; a very clear sense of what posthuman security and IR might mean. We could push this question even further and ask if the increased frequency by which digital, algorithmically driven, cognitive artefacts[24] are integrated into already ecological (think gut microbiota) cognitive and decision-making processes poses a threat to the stability of the equilibrium that we refer to (often normatively) as human subjectivity? Does the introduction of the technologies grouped under the umbrella into the ecology of human subjectivity place certain capacities at risk? Do new capacities emerge, what is the trade off? This seems like a case for the Turing Police. It seems likely that this is not a purely speculative question. There are numerous experiments testing if sensory substitution devices (SSDs) can become part of extended cognitive systems (e.g. Hurley and Noë 2003; Bach-y-Rita and Kercel 2003; Dotov, Nie, and Chemero 2010). The experiments have shown that in fact sensory-substitution devices can become part of extended cognitive systems and additionally these artefacts partially constitute the extended cognitive system. This reinforces Leroi-Gourhan's much earlier point. The point, coarsely, is that cognitive artefacts do not always remain stand-apart supports for human cognitive systems, but rather become aspects of cognitive ecologies, thus transforming them. If, as Leroi-Gourhan argues, this is not new, but the very definition of the human, then our main concern is not necessarily whether these new forms of hybridity mark a break between the human and the

---

[24] Cognitive artifacts are devices designed to maintain, display, or operate upon information in order to serve a representational function and that affect human cognitive performance (Norman 1991).

posthuman; indeed by this account we have always been posthuman. The question is if and how ecologies which sustain things that we value about human subjectivity are altered and in what ways.

Perhaps in asking about the relation between the discourses about posthumanism, the human subject, IR, security and the existential challenges created by climate change and the Anthropocene – the constellation of concepts that this volume bravely takes on – there is a choice to be had: work towards securing the ecological/centrifugal subject as a rational and also potentially caring actor capable of at least tying to address the existential security challenges posed by the Anthropocene or admit that the planetary system (Gaia) would be better off without human beings or human subjects. In other words, if we accept the centrifugal notion of the subject that I propose, and also the centrality of human subjectivity to any discussion of politics that we can fathom; then we should try to maintain within this ecological picture the subjective capacities that we care about and which we will undoubtedly need to address the ecological challenges facing the planet. These seem to me to be the two epistemologically coherent options. The notion of the posthuman considered in biological or even functional terms is of course interesting and important, but it is not what is paramount here, since it is – I contend – the human subject and not just the human that matters to politics (IR and security included) properly speaking. The idea of post-subjective IR or security is not something that I think we as subjects can say anything about.

References

Bach-y-Rita Paul and Stephen W. Kercel. 2003. Sensory substitution and the human-machine interface. *Trends in Cognitive Sciences* 7(12): 541-546.

Benatar, David. 2006. *Better Never to Have Been: the Harm of Coming into Existence*. Oxford: Claredon Press.

Boyd, Danah and Kate Crawford. 2011. Six Provocations for Big Data, A Decade in Internet Time: Symposium on the Dynamics of the Internet and Society, September 2011. Available at SSRN: http://dx.doi.org/10.2139/ssrn.1926431. Accessed 17 May 2017.

Danaher, John. 2016. "The Threat of Algocracy: Reality, Resistance and Accommodation"*Philosophy and Technology* 29(3): 245-268.

Dobromir G. Dotov, Lin Nie and Anthony Chemero. 2010. A Demonstration of the Transition from Ready-to-Hand to Unready-to-Hand. *PLoS ONE 5(3)*, e9433.

Evrensel, Alper and Mehmet E. Ceylan. 2015. "The Gut-Brain Axis: The Missing Link in Depression" *Clinical Psychopharmacology and Neuroscience*, 13(3): 239–244.

Gibson, William. 1984. *Neuromancer*. New York: Acebooks.

Hull, David. 1980. "On Human Nature" *Environmental Ethics* 2 (1): 81-88

Hurley, Susan and Alva Noë. 2003. "Neural plasticity and consciousness" *Biology and Philosophy,* 18: 131-168.

Kant, Immanuel. 1784. *Beantwortung der Frage: Was ist Aufklärung? Berlinische Monatsschrift* Friedrich Gedike and Johann Erich Biester (eds.) December 1784 edition. Available online at: https://www.marxists.org/reference/subject/ethics/kant/enlightenment.htm. Accessed 17 May 2017.

Leroi-Gourhan, A. 1973. *Evolution et Techniques II - Milieu et Techniques,* 2d edition, Paris: Albin Michel

Mitchell, Audra. 2014. Only Human: A worldly approach to security. *Security Dialogue*, 45(1), 5-21

Norman, Donald. 1991. Cognitive Artifacts. In: J.M. Carrol (ed.) *Designing Interaction: Psychology at the Human Computer Interface*. Cambridge: Cambridge University Press.

Roden, David. 2015. *Posthuman Life: Philosophy at the Edge of the Human*. Abingdon: Routledge.

Soutou, Georges-Henri. 2000. Was There a European Order in the Twentieth Century? From the Concert of Europe to the End of the Cold War. *Contemporary European History*. Theme Issue: Reflections on the Twentieth Century. 9 (3), 330.

Turney, Jon. 2016. *Beyond cell wars. Aeon* 28th March 2016. Available online at: https://aeon.co/essays/why-we-should-guard-against-military-notions-of-immunity. Accessed 14 May 2017.

Walker, R. B. J. 1993. *Inside/Outside: International Relations as Political Theory.* Cambridge: Cambridge University Press.

Note on Indexing

E-IR's publications do not feature indexes due to the prohibitive costs of assembling them. If you are reading this book in paperback and want to find a particular word or phrase you can do so by downloading a free PDF version of this book from the E-IR website.

View the e-book in any standard PDF reader such as Adobe Acrobat Reader (pc) or Preview (mac) and enter your search terms in the search box. You can then navigate through the search results and find what you are looking for. In practice, this method can prove much more targeted and effective than consulting an index.

If you are using apps (or devices) such as iBooks or Kindle to read our e-books, you should also find word search functionality in those.

You can find all of our e-books at: http://www.e-ir.info/publications

Printed in Great Britain
by Amazon